Sacred Creativity

Sacred Creativity

RECLAIM THE JOY OF YOUR GOD-GIVEN GIFTS FOR HIS GLORY

Jena Holliday

WATERBROOK

ISBN 978-0-593-58147-6

Published in the United States by WaterBrook, an imprint of Random House, a division of Penguin Random House LLC.

WATERBROOK and colophon are registered trademarks of Penguin Random House LLC.

Printed in China

First Edition

waterbrookmultnomah.com

2 4 6 8 9 7 5 3 1

SPECIAL SALES

Most WaterBrook and Ink & Willow books are available at special quantity discounts when purchased in bulk by corporations, organizations, and special-interest groups. Custom imprinting or excerpting can also be done to fit special needs. For information, please email specialmarketscms@penguinrandomhouse.com.

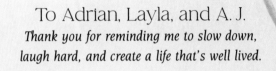

To Adrian, Layla, and A. J.
*Thank you for reminding me to slow down,
laugh hard, and create a life that's well lived.*

To my parents, Kandy and Wade
*Thank you for teaching me that I can
do anything with a little bit of faith.*

To each of my siblings
*Thank you for always being by my side
to help make both messes and
masterpieces in the name of creativity.*

Table of Contents

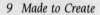

Made to Create

Ok God, I'm going to do it.

I sat staring at my phone. On it was an illustration I had just finished drawing days before. I was planning to share it on Instagram, which I had done many times with other pieces. But this time felt different. The drawing itself was of a dark-skinned Black woman, standing in a field of wildflowers. Her vibrantly colored headband held back her fluffy dark brown fro. She was dressed in a beautiful tan blouse and wore a pair of pink dangly earrings. The words "Do It As Worship" were written in the sky as she looked out ahead of her.

As I stared at the image, I could feel my stomach drop. It was as if butterflies were flying around in there. My throat suddenly felt extremely dry as I tried to swallow. I closed my eyes and hit Publish. With my eyes closed, I exhaled, "I'm doing this." The post went onto my Instagram page and along with it came a flood of emotions. I reread my caption a few times, checking that it was clear and free of any errors I could have missed. My words and this image were out there for everyone to see and read. I was really doing this.

It hadn't been an easy road though. The path that I had taken to get there had been difficult and lonely and untraditional, but I had found my own way and had figured out a lot of things on my own, and I wanted to share it with others. I felt the desire to help other women, especially women of color, lean into their creativity. I didn't see many women that looked like me pursuing creative careers in illustration. Of course, there were some, but not enough to make me feel that the art world would have room for more of us—room for me. Women of color weren't the ones getting all of the attention, big contracts, or promotions as mentors.

My experience, as an artist and small-business owner of Spoonful of Faith, taught me that running hard enough, working long enough, or fighting my way up the ranks wasn't the road for me. I knew that end of the route only held burnout. Somewhere in my journey, I had gained the confidence to find my artistic voice and share it with others. Not the voice the world had painted for me as a Black artist, but the voice and message that felt uniquely mine. I had figured out how to have courage in being exactly who God created me to be. Black, loving, free, soft, bold, and joyous. That voice was mine; it was unlike any other, and it was made in the image of the Creator.

But my heart had also seen so many other women like me who had struggled to find their footing. So many with potential and creative gifts that didn't know how to walk forward. Women who, like me, didn't feel seen or didn't know the way. Women who were bubbling with ideas and creativity but felt there was no room in this world for what they were given to share. Why did it have to be such a long and treacherous process for us?

For about two years I sat with the idea that I needed to do something to chart a healthy way forward for budding creators. Not in the hustle-and-grind kind of way but in a way that encourages them to create from a place that feels free and authentic and is led by faith, instead of driven by sales, productivity, or accolades. Deep in my heart, I felt the responsibility and desire to share what I'd learned with others, but I didn't think I had time to add this to my never-ending to-do list.

During this same time, I was fielding text messages from girlfriends and emails from strangers asking me how I showed up with confidence, doing something that

You are Creative by faith.

Do it as
worship

felt so authentic to me and that seemed like it was working for me. I had fellow entrepreneurs tell me they had been struggling to find their voice and show up more confidently in the sea of social media and algorithms. They felt like they couldn't keep their heads above water. Women I would meet at events would tell me they simply didn't feel like they were creative or that they even trusted in their creativity. I knew I had to extend a hand to other creatives who felt stuck, lonely, or unsure in their path, just like I had been.

My post with the official announcement starting a small online community and course called Do It as Worship was up. I read and reread my caption, waiting to see how my community would respond. I was relieved. I'd done it. I'd put it out there, trusting that God would reveal the next steps for nurturing the women He would bring into this community. My nerves turned to excitement for what was ahead.

Over the next few months, I walked side by side with women across the country. Brick by brick we built a creative community. We shared hopes and dreams and comforted one another through fears and setbacks. We wrestled with creative blocks and juggling priorities. I'd have moments of overwhelm, feeling like I had taken on way too much, then I'd witness times where someone would have breakthrough. I saw women who had for so long felt shut down and silenced find a safe place to be open and heard again. Women who had never shared their dreams shared them with me in this special place. The community was a place of encouragement where women pushed through fears, became unstuck, released the pressure to perform, and used the wonderfully unique gifts that were inside them. One by one, they began to recognize their uniqueness and figure out their way forward.

One woman shared her struggles as a creative: "I have found myself lost in my identity as the suggestions of others clouded my judgment as to what I should be creating and doing with my gifts." In comparing herself to others, she became confused about

what to do with her creative gifts. Through this group she discovered her work was never equal to her worth. She found power in the act of creating simply to create—as a way to honor the gift and the Giver. She experienced freedom that she hadn't felt before. The work God was doing in all of us through connection and community brought tears to my eyes.

I watched and witnessed image bearers open their mouths, speak life into the things they had been called to do, and create. Many of them gained confidence to walk forward, to show up exactly as God created them to be. No longer afraid, no longer comparing—but free to be.

And that is my prayer for you as you read the words in this book. I want you to find freedom, joy, and confidence to use your creative gifts, too.

I want to be a mentor for you. The mentor I wish I had early in my career, reminding me that in the same way that God made me one-of-a-kind, God had given me the ability to make something that is one-of-a-kind. God invited me to "create by faith," as I like to say. By tapping into that well of creativity, I could have impact beyond my wildest dreams.

God can use your creativity, too.

Maybe you've started believing the lie that you aren't creative. Or maybe you feel that what you have to offer is not enough. Maybe you've always doubted that what God gave you was enough or that it could be used in a way that encourages your people or those around you. Maybe, like me, the spark used to be there, and life blew it out.

This book is your invitation to join me in discovering how you can take your God-given gifts and use them in confidence and joyful worship. As you create by faith—picking up your brushes, your pens, your hands—you'll discover that God wants to teach, love, and transform you and the lives around you.

As you read, my hope is that the words and stories release you and your heart from the burden of producing, the pressure to perform, to be perfect, or have it all figured out. Instead, I hope you grow in confidence, knowing that you can just show

good things grow slow

up as your unique self, with what you've been given, and experience freedom and joy as you create.

At the end of each section of this book, you'll find creative challenges, a playlist, reflection questions, and an affirmation. All of these I offer in the hope that they will propel you forward as your creativity blooms and flourishes. Take your time walking through the book, reflecting on your own journey as you learn from mine, making space for new thoughts and ideas to emerge, and finding encouragement and motivation to create.

When we make room for Him in the way we create, our gifts will make room for God's blessing to cover us in more ways than we can imagine.

Okay, friend, let's do this!

You are at the beginning of a new adventure with God. Take a moment to breathe in the excitement and beauty of beginnings. As you breathe out, release your expectations. Stay open to His leading and guiding as you explore your creative gifts. Speak life as you begin to create something new.

The One Who Created You

WHEN I WAS growing up, my family hardly ever missed church on Sunday. Because my father was one of the ministers, most of the time you would catch my mom, brothers, sisters, and me in church whenever the doors were open. Having a front row seat to church life meant I saw miracles. I saw life transformations, but I also saw when people were not authentic. I saw people who were one way in front of the church and another way outside of the church. I promised myself that I wasn't going to be "that person." I was going to strive to live the straight and narrow path I heard preached. I tried not to make mistakes or deviate from the rules and norms.

The combination of growing up in a legalistic church culture, having strict parents, and my own rule-following, people-pleasing personality meant I strived to do everything "right." I had exceptional grades, sang solos in church and school choir, was liked by my teachers, ran track, and was a competitive cheerleader. I was the "good girl" who did what she was supposed to do and didn't get in trouble.

If you're anything like I was, you've probably found yourself trying to do everything right, so you don't disappoint anyone. It can so easily create an unnecessary burden that stifles our lives, including our gifts and creativity. Faith isn't meant to do that,

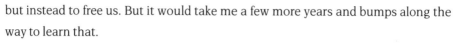

but instead to free us. But it would take me a few more years and bumps along the way to learn that.

By junior year of high school, I felt stifled by my parents' rules and the religious standards. As an adult, I understand why my parents had rules and structure—after all, with seven children, they needed some way to keep the chaos to a minimum. But, sixteen-year-old me just wanted a later curfew. *I always do the right thing*, I thought. *Why won't my parents give me more freedom?*

Trying to keep up with the rules and expectations became a heavy burden to carry.

Though I witnessed evidence of God being real, my experience with God had not felt personal. God always seemed to be moving in someone *else's* life. I was here, doing all the right things, I thought, but where was God? I didn't feel Him near like others did. And because I was determined to be authentic, I wasn't going to pretend or lie and say I felt something I didn't feel.

"If You're real, show me," I would pray. And I didn't see anything change. I was exhausted in my efforts to live up to my perfect standards, while having no personal relationship with God. If God was real, He was going to have to reciprocate the effort and make Himself known in my life. I wanted to really experience what others talked about. I wanted something real and something personal, and I would wait for it to come and not force it.

I started counting down the days to graduation and my eighteenth birthday. I wanted to be free to make my own decisions, and that day would come when I moved out of state to go to college.

I was excited to live my life, have the most fun possible, and not think about the big questions. I was looking forward to being on my own, away from my parents, living by my own rules, and making my own choices. And did I ever. I spent most of my nights partying way too late, pulling all-nighters in the computer lab, and suffering from hangovers in class the next morning.

After the first year, out-of-state tuition got expensive, so I moved back to Minnesota to finish college at a school I could commute to. I was working a good job, going to

You made the stars and know me by name

open hearts & open hands

school full-time, and living my young care-free life. I started dating a man I really loved and would later marry. I still enjoyed planning fun nights out with friends but after I graduated, I was in the full-time corporate world, working a big-girl job in retail merchandising. On the outside, things looked good with my career, my relationships, and my financial situation. But, on the inside, I began questioning my purpose and my future. I had absorbed all the culture's messages about what a successful twenty-something life should look like. I'd done it, yet I couldn't shake the feeling that I wasn't fulfilled. With all I had, something felt missing.

Have you experienced that feeling? Where you reached a long-time goal and then felt . . . empty? I know now that there are places in our hearts that only God can fill, but back then I was still searching. Yet, God pursued me and had plans to reach me through the passion He had already placed inside of me: creativity.

It was during that time I thought that maybe I just needed a creative outlet. My job was data driven and I analyzed sales and worked with spreadsheets all day. So, I started a fashion and lifestyle blog where I would share my outfit of the day and a little about my life.

As I sat at home on my tan couch in the townhome, talking to my boyfriend, I wondered and asked out loud, "Is this all life has to give?" Admittedly, it was the dead of winter in Minnesota. It's not unusual to question your whole life when the days are short, there's very little sunlight, and the temperatures are less than 20 degrees for weeks. But this was different. The thoughts and questions about where my path was heading consumed me. I couldn't put my finger on exactly what I needed or why I urgently needed an answer. There was a weight on my heart.

It felt like life was all work and I had barely any time to live and enjoy my life. The thought that running the rat race, climbing the corporate ladder, and living for the weekend or a vacation was all I had to look forward to for the next twenty, thirty, forty years felt so sad. The fog of confusion and dissatisfaction followed me everywhere. I tried to relax my mind and often turned to unhealthy self-medicating in times of stress. After trying everything I knew to help me chill out, I finally went to lie down.

Hours later, around four in the morning, I woke up. The room was dark, but my mind was clearer than anything I had ever experienced. A voice in my heart and mind so clearly said, *Why are you asking everyone else where to go, who to be, and what do to, except the One who created you?*

The words washed over my heart and sunk into my spirit, like something I had never felt before. Peace filled me, and I knew without a doubt it was a moment with God. Immediately my eyes filled with tears, my worries fell to the ground, and the confusion that had plagued me left. The God I had been wondering about finally felt so real.

It was like nothing I had ever experienced in all my life. I am not gonna lie, I had a moment of doubt, asking, *Am I imagining this? Or maybe still dreaming?*

But I knew deep down this wasn't a dream. And something in me changed. I hadn't considered that God, my Creator, would have insight and answers for my troubled heart. I had never heard anything so crystal clear, and I wanted to find out more about the One who created me.

Somewhere deep within my heart had been touched. The girl who had constantly been asking for direction, permission, and purpose but couldn't find it had finally heard from the very Source of all creation. I never expected to hear from God. I had not been attending church, studying my Bible, or praying. Yet God did what God does. He met me where I was and invited me to a lasting and life-changing relationship.

That night, with a refreshed perspective, I felt a closeness like never before to a God I had only read about. I wasn't fearful and I felt no pressure, only love and clarity. Although I didn't know what my next step would be, I finally knew Who to follow. That moment would also be the first step to showing up as my full self without holding back my gifts, ideas, or abilities and actively using them just as God made me to do.

That experience was a catalyst for me to step out in faith. I sat in the knowledge that God was my Creator and He loved me. He intricately made me and purposefully placed gifts within my hands to be used for His glory. Recognizing this, I began to see my self-confidence soar. I began to hope for the future. Knowing I had someone who had more answers than I did helped me take the pressure off my shoulders a little. It encouraged me to have faith, and soon I began believing bigger and seeing potential around me.

I didn't know it, but that moment was the first step of a new exploration of myself as a creation of God's.

How has faith helped you tap into your passions, gifts, and abilities? Or do you find that you sometimes still push them away? If you are like I was, it might be time to reconnect with the One who gave you these gifts. That was such a vital part of my journey.

Each day thereafter, I'd show up to my dining room table with my notebook, pen, Bible, and coffee and talk to God. I would clench my eyes shut and whisper, hopeful He was listening, "I just want this to be real, and I'm going to be honest with you." Tears would fall from my eyes. I wanted something true. I felt He knew that, too. This time with God felt like a big warm blanket wrapped itself around me, assuring and affirming me that I was safe here. I felt as if God really wanted me just as I was, flaws and all. I'd never been more sure of it.

I never knew what these sessions would look like, but I'd be ready for where He'd take me. It's worth taking that time.

Some days I'd feel a push to read scriptures or listen to a teaching on my phone. Sometimes I'd get bored and feel an eagerness to write, draw, or rearrange my home. My mission was that I'd bring my full self and get to know God. My hope was that He'd show me the way. Every day as I showed up, I'd trust just a little bit more of who God was.

What happened next took me by complete surprise. As I would pray or journal, questions in my heart began to form around the creative gifts I had locked up years ago. In gentle whispers, God was asking me:

What are your dreams?
Why did you stop dreaming?
Why did you stop drawing?
Why don't you think your writing is good or impactful?
Why don't you share your heart more?
Why do you doubt what is in you?

As much as this was a journey to creativity, it was a journey through dealing with some of my roadblocks to putting my trust in God. I had to do some internal work in the process of exploring my creativity. *Why had I stopped dreaming, drawing, and creating?*

My art and the business that would emerge years later came from my heart and soul—a deep place that God was molding and shaping, holding me, pushing me, guiding me. It all started with Him.

Creative isn't something we have to become. It is a gift we get to tap into and use. Perhaps, like me, you've felt unfulfilled trying to be something you were never meant to be. Take a minute to hear from the One who created you. What creative avenue is God prompting you to explore? For me, it was visual art. For you, it could be cooking or baking, writing, decorating your home, doing photography, or doing hair. Make a note of what you think it is for you.

You already have it in you, friend.

And as we'd do with any gift, we get to receive it, unwrap it, and make use of it whenever we desire. Creativity is the Creator's gift to each of us, and God loves when we connect to that part of ourselves.

"Creativity is the Creator's gift to each of us."

Rejoice in Small Beginnings

I WAS ROCKING back and forth and nursing my five-month-old baby girl, Layla. The chair made an eerie squeaking noise that brought me back to the traumatic experience we had endured to get Layla here. I had been in labor for hours, but Layla just wouldn't come down. My water had already broken, and the doctors were worried that it was taking too long for me to dilate. We soon found out the position she was in was blocking her from getting through. My heart tensed as the doctors told me the new plan. It was time for an emergency cesarean.

In the operating room, I vividly remember the moment I saw Layla's face. My world stood still. All the waiting and mental exhaustion we experienced to get to this place washed away. My eyes welled as my husband, Adrian, and I looked at her and then each other. Pure joy. I yelled out that I wanted another one and everyone in the OR laughed at my comment. It was probably the morphine talking, but there was certainly joy. We had done it. We knew things had changed right there in an instant. Officially holding our baby girl. We were in new territory, in a brand-new beginning.

Before Layla, I had always been such a go-getter. My calendar was packed with social events, me time, and, because I liked variety in my work, more than one job.

That middle-of-the-night encounter with God changed me forever, but my life was still going full speed on the outside. In the two years following that night, I had been promoted to an assistant buyer in a demanding job doing retail merchandising for beauty products. My life was full, managing a growing fashion blog, planning a wedding, keeping up with friends and family, and excitedly expecting a baby.

Those days were marked by spiritual growth, continuing a real relationship versus a ritual relationship with my Creator. God and I had our own rituals in the morning with coffee as I explored the Bible. I had a renewed perspective on the Scriptures. I allowed myself to question and explore. I was free in Jesus in a way that ten-year-old me could never have imagined.

But in those first months of motherhood, I quickly realized it was not my show anymore; our daughter was the priority, and she was going to tell us what was up. It was beautiful, terrifying, and also full of waves of loss and grief over the season of life I was departing.

After five months of this new season, I sat in my rocking chair and finally felt a moment of togetherness. There was stillness, but also a gentle stirring. Something had shifted in my heart during this season. As I nursed Layla, I thought, *I have to be an example for her*. I didn't know exactly how that would play out, but I knew I wanted my daughter to be confident in who she was and in using the gifts that God would give her. So, I decided I needed to do the same in my life. As I looked around me, I saw dozens of things I wanted to try and no clue where to start. Yet my desire to lead Layla ignited a new determination within me to figure it out. I wanted to walk forward no matter what I faced. I was at a new beginning and finally felt a renewed strength and energy to move forward.

Perhaps you are at a new beginning in your life. Maybe you're experimenting in your creativity, new to motherhood, in a new relationship or a new job, or possibly moving to a new city or home. Beginning something new can often be exciting, but the heaviness of not knowing what is to come might weigh you down. You might feel uncertainty about how long the journey will take or stress about all the work that will be involved.

For me, it was the fear of not knowing what I was doing or what was ahead. I had been away from using my art and creativity publicly for so long, that I knew there was work to be done. I also felt like I didn't have much to begin with. I didn't have a fancy art degree; I didn't have expensive tools or supplies or an audience who liked my work. I had a calling from God, His promise to be with me, and the gifts He had placed inside. I had a baby on my hip and determination in my heart. Was it enough? I honestly wasn't sure it was. It felt like a small and humble place to begin.

What if I told you that God delights in your new beginnings? That He rejoices to see you begin? It might feel difficult to believe it, but He does. And there is a story in the Bible that I have held on to over the years that has reminded me of this truth.

> Do not despise these small beginnings, for the Lord rejoices to see work begin, to see the plumb line in Zerubbabel's hand.
>
> —Zechariah 4:10 (NLT)

Have you ever heard of Zerubbabel? If not, he was a descendant of David who was born in Babylon during the exile of Judeans. Eventually he became a leader and the head of the tribe of Judah. During this time, King Cyrus II commanded the Jews to return to Judah, where they would restore and rebuild Solomon's temple. When Zerubabbel and the tribe arrived and began building the foundation for the temple, he was ridiculed by the elders about how he was building it. The size of the temple wasn't big enough for them and would be much smaller than the great temple that Solomon built. They compared him to those before him. He faced distractions and constant hindrances that held up the process to get the temple completed. After sixteen years of obstacles—yeah, sixteen years—Zerubabbel was finally able to start rebuilding the temple again. But picking it up again was discouraging. The finish line still looked so far away.

In the story, we see God doesn't abandon His people or Zerubbabel. In his time of uncertainty, Zerubbabel receives a message from an angel of God to encourage his heart and bring hope and clarity as he begins again.

God saw Zerubbabel's small beginning and his efforts and there was nothing to hate or despise about that moment. Instead, God rejoiced that Zerubabbel had begun the work.

"The Lord rejoices to see the work begin." Read that again. God rejoices when we begin our work. I couldn't believe it the first time I read it. I tried to picture God rejoicing. Jumping up and down giddy to see me at my house in sweats, tired, babywearing with a paintbrush in my hand. I pictured Him cheering me on as I stole a few minutes to write in my journal while my daughter napped. My Creator delighted in those moments.

Can you imagine it? God taking great pleasure in seeing you draw scribbles in your sketchpad or write the first paragraph of that story you've had locked inside. He delights in the first cake you've baked in a while or the first lyrics you write for a song that's been stuck in your mind. Take a moment to envision God rejoicing over your beginning. His joy as you take your first baby steps forward. He is pleased not that it's finished, but that it has begun. How powerful and utterly refreshing is that?

Believing that God rejoices in the start can require a little faith, though, can't it? It can be tough to believe that anything is even happening if we can't see the evidence. We often need proof on paper, a check marked on our to-do list, a report to prove there's progress in what we're pursuing. It's hard to wrap our heads around the fact that there is anything worth rejoicing when we are staring at a blank page or standing at the starting line. Yet God rejoices even in those moments:

He rejoices in you showing up.
He rejoices in your messy sketches.
He rejoices in your brainstorm session.
He rejoices in your new recipe idea.
He rejoices in your scribbled-down Post-it notes for the book that's within you.

Trust that there is delight in your stirring. There is hope and joy in the first steps. Knowing that can bring release and the confidence you need to show up, open your hands, and begin walking out those first moments of a new venture.

You don't have to wait until everything is perfect. Don't overthink it. Just take the first small step.

Even if you don't have hours to dedicate to your craft, make a plan to carve out small moments in your day to tap into the creativity you have inside. Here are a few different things you can try to get started.

GO DEEPER

I didn't have much solo time to dedicate early on, but I had lots of time as I nursed and took care of my daughter to make the time to think. The first step was easy for me and that was to simply think about what was on my heart to do. What were my hopes, my God-given gifts, and things I was passionate about? How did those connect to what I felt God nudging me toward? What did I love? What did I care deeply for? What came naturally? What did others who came to me always ask me for? What was something that if I started talking about it, I couldn't shut up? So many of these things, I had overlooked, but they were tiny breadcrumbs, a trail to help me tap further into who God had made me to be and how that might come out of me. These are great questions to ask yourself!

DAYDREAM AND BRAINSTORM

The very next step was to daydream. I did this during Layla's nap time. I allowed myself to dream with God. Instead of keeping the thoughts in my head, I wrote them down. I didn't know what exactly I wanted to do, but I knew I loved to draw and create, and I loved to encourage and inspire others, too. I bought a notebook and used it for my ideas, thoughts, and dreams. I wrote down all my thoughts about what I wanted to do. No idea was too big or too small. There was something powerful in writing them out in my notebook. No one had to see them but me and God. Getting them onto paper made the ideas seem more tangible. This helped me feel like they weren't so far away anymore. It also allowed me to begin opening my mind to dream of the possibilities and be childlike again. I invite you to do the same: Grab a journal or open a note on your phone and get to writing down those dreams and ideas.

GET GRANULAR

The last step that helped was about getting granular in how I moved forward.

To get granular, think of what you are beginning and ask how you can begin right now. What do you need in this moment to do it? For me, I needed to go into my garage and find that box of art supplies. I needed to do a physical inventory of what I had on hand and what I needed to start. That was the only thing I added to my weekly task list. Breaking it down into small, daily (or weekly), actionable steps made it easier to move forward confidently. Momentum builds momentum, and soon enough, I was actually creating!

What might your first step be? Perhaps it's making time in your calendar to dream. Or taking out your kitchen tools so they are in view for you to use the next time you have a moment. Maybe it's leaving the paints on your desk where you can easily make some marks on paper when you walk by. Or calling up a friend to do a little brainstorm session with you.

Whatever your first step, remember the Lord rejoices to see the work begin. If you've put it down, He rejoices to see you pick it back up again. It doesn't have to be big or fully planned out. Just know He is delighted to see you start, and He will walk with you to carry it out to completion. Let that truth inspire you to stay the course. It may be hard for you to see it, but trust that your Creator sees ahead and where you are going.

"Momentum builds momentum."

mercy
triumphs
over
judgment
James 2:13

What's Holding You Back?

What are your dreams?
Why did you stop dreaming?
Why did you stop drawing?
Why don't you think your writing is good or impactful?
Why don't you share your heart more?
Why do you doubt what is in you?

Even after my faith became real and I'd restarted my creative journey, I still wrestled with these questions.

That fact is, I'd never considered myself an artist. Growing up, I was always just a girl who loved to use her imagination and make things. Creativity was highly encouraged in our household. When boredom came, my mom and dad left it up to my six siblings and me to figure out how to spend our time. My older sisters and I loved to craft and make things from scratch.

As far back as I can remember, we were making our own Barbie clothes, styling their hair, and painting their nails. We'd make our own furniture out of cardboard for their houses and craft old clothes for the wardrobes. If we didn't have something we needed, we'd look for supplies to make a handmade version of it ourselves. During our teen years, my older sister Bianca would come to me with ideas for clothes she had found in magazines or on blogs, and we'd spend our weekends trying to re-create them.

Creativity has always been a part of who I am. I didn't even have to be good at it or be the best. I was simply excited I got to be creative.

But a shift started when I got into middle school. I loved art and was so excited to take an elective art class for the semester. Although it was my favorite part of the week, I noticed something within me change. When I was surrounded by my peers in class, I began to doubt my gifts. Instead of the excitement I shared with my sister when we created, I felt fear and comparison rise within me. Instead of the pleasure of creating, I felt this immense pressure to be a good artist, to be better than others, and to do everything without mistake. When I saw my art displayed next to my peers', I picked apart everything I made. What if I failed? What if I was told my art needed work or received a bad grade?

Have you been there?

I had never felt the need to compare my creativity to anyone before, but now doubt paralyzed me. What if I simply wasn't cut out to make and create art like I thought I was? Fear started to consume my gift and worth.

During class one afternoon my friends and I chatted about what it might look like to be professional artists. We talked about going to school for art and how cool it would be to pursue it for a living. My art teacher, standing close by, overheard our conversation and from her body language, we knew she wanted to chime in. Her response still surprises me to this day.

As she looked at our table of twelve-year-olds, with worry in her eyes, she told us that we'd be better off going to school for business, not attending art school. You could hear the disappointment in her voice, like she'd made that mistake herself and

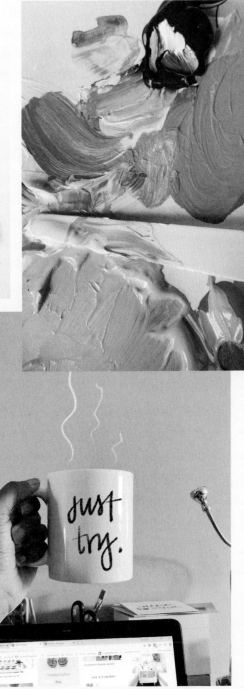

*"Be willing
to try
new things."*

didn't want us to follow in her shoes. Even though she may have meant well, at the time all I could hear was that I wasn't good enough. I didn't realize until I was older how people can sometimes project their own fears and perceived failures onto others, even kids. But that one conversation changed my perspective on where I would focus my time and education. The seed of fear and doubt I had already been experiencing by taking this class got watered yet again.

I made up my mind that she was probably right. I only created or practiced DIY projects from the comfort of home. That light had dimmed, and I stopped sharing with people outside of my family and close friends—people I trusted. While I still used creativity in smaller ways, I stopped taking public art classes or any art class offered through my school. It was way too scary for me.

My confidence in sharing my gifts deflated, and I stuck to drawing doodles in the margins of my notebooks or on my homework pages. Even when I'd get notes on my doodles from the teachers when they graded my work, telling me "Great drawing!" fear would overshadow the moment. The gift that was once so easily used now felt locked up. It would take years for me to realize how that encounter in middle school caused me to limit my ideas of who I was and what I could do. I downplayed and even hid my abilities, my dreams, and what I thought was possible. It wasn't until God explicitly asked me, *Why are you asking everyone else where to go, who to be, and what to do, except the One who created you?* that I was able to start recalling times when I had unknowingly allowed doubt to keep me grounded, unable to fly.

Sometimes someone's offhand remark or response can cause us to stop using our gifts or doubt what is within. Have you found yourself asking similar questions like the ones I asked myself at the start of this chapter? Take some time to sit with moments that caused you doubt and fear.

As I sat with those questions, I got to the heart of what I had been believing about myself. I had been hurt in places I hadn't realized. The sting left me hesitant to get back up and try again. I quit dreaming because I didn't believe there was anything to gain from my dreams. I didn't create because I didn't think I was as good as everyone else or that it even mattered to the purpose of my life. But there is something special about every bit of what God placed in me. My Creator wanted me to be confident in every part of myself. So, I took a deep breath. It was time to move forward into an adventure—this time, exploring my gifts.

I felt prompted to try new things, to openly explore art and creativity again. To take the time to explore my heart, to share my words, to freely create and use what was already in me.

Be willing to try new things. I did, and I'm so thankful for all that I learned about myself during that time. It helped take the pressure off myself, and I kept my mind open to trying unfamiliar activities. I tried being creative in the kitchen. I tried sewing. I even considered playing an instrument, since learning the guitar was always a secret desire of mine. What followed that series of trying new things was refreshing. There is something special about trying. It comes not with heavy expectations but with an invitation asking you to be present and open. That was it. It was the introduction into a new world of cultivating my creativity without pressure. This new mindset of "trying" allowed me to grow more freely and confidently.

The more I tried things, the more I thought about picking my art back up. Just as I was starting to be open to the idea, I immediately had an opportunity to use my art again. One afternoon following a Sunday church service, an older sister from our congregation came up to me with a gift. As I opened it, I saw a small ceramic dish with a lid on it. Inside were cards with words printed on each side. As I examined it, I noticed that some held scriptures and some were affirming phrases.

When I got it home, I set the dish on my desk. I didn't really know what I'd do with it. I wondered if I could do something creative with the cards, and that's when the idea hit me. I took out one card and mulled over the words on it. I began to draw an illustration of a woman sitting beside it. *Maybe this could be a fun creative practice,* I thought. I kept at it. Whenever I'd have a little time, I'd pull a card and draw a woman to go along with it. I must say that, looking back, the illustrations aren't that great. Okay, really, they were stick figures. That's how I learned to draw bodies—with stick figures. I had the faces' part down after doodling so many for years, but the bodies were sticks. I also couldn't draw eyes. When I'd draw them, they were often crossed or looking in the wrong directions, so I just closed them altogether. Years later, the closed eyes would become a signature of my style!

I began capturing photos of the drawings I made and posting them on my personal Instagram account. I'd add a little caption explaining the idea or thought for each drawing and a little encouragement to whoever was reading. That small decision to try new things and stay open with my creativity sparked a new desire to practice my art again. I'd find myself drawing during slow meetings at work, or on phone calls, or even on my breaks.

I also started to get small reminders that I was on the right path. Sometimes it was a friend or loved one sharing how one of my posts encouraged them, or it was the deep feeling of joy I had never experienced until I spent dedicated time creating. It was also about making something I thought wasn't great, sharing it anyway, and having that drawing connect to someone or be just what they needed at that time. Every tiny moment was the breeding ground for strengthening my creative practice and for building up my creative confidence.

God wants to walk with you in exploring everything within you. Your heart, your mind, and even your gifts. He cares about the whole of you and how He's designed you to be. Those hidden parts, you know, the ones you've tucked away? Well, those might also carry purpose or be used in powerful ways when you let them out. You are never too far along to try. To face new things. To explore new places.

It can feel like a lofty step to explore new things. When will I find time? How will I begin? You might even doubt that you're good enough or have the energy to give what it needs. Maybe, like me, you didn't think any of this mattered to God. Well, you can do it with small steps forward.

Here are a few simple ways to get moving:

First, it's good to explore some of those internal questions. Take a moment to sit and think of the way God made you and the purpose that might be within. Here's a starting point of questions that might help you to explore inside:

- What is something you've dreamed of?
- Why did you stop _____?
- Why don't you think your _____ is good or impactful?
- Why don't you share your heart more?
- Why do you doubt what is in you?

While not all of these may apply to your particular story, they can be a starting point for you to reflect. Try adding your own and take an honest inventory of your responses. Digging in may help guide you to where you need to begin as you embark on your next creative journey.

Next, remember the art of trying. Sit down and make a list of things you felt held back from that you now feel a push to start. Then add things you have maybe always desired to try. Try to list as many things as possible. Then, take one thing from your list and plan to try it.

Treat each new thing you want to do as an experiment. The fun part about an experiment is that you get to lead with curiosity. You can attempt to make an educated guess, but you must go through with the experiment to see the final results. No matter the outcome, you won't be wrong. There is less pressure for you to get it right, just a chance to gather data and new ideas.

The process of trying helped me walk with wonder instead of fear. It opened my mind and allowed me to step out and start sharing more of my words and drawings, first through my blog and later a small Etsy shop.

Although I was constantly questioning if I was on the right path, I kept trusting day by day. It is important to keep your eyes peeled for confirmation that you are on the right path, or the markers along the way.

Do you feel a deep sense of joy or excitement as you are exploring? Maybe a word of encouragement or confirmation from a friend? Perhaps as you pray, you are filled with more ideas of ways to create and express God's love? As you stay open and explore the gifts within you, make a mental note or journal the moments that encourage you. This can be helpful to strengthen your creative gift and practice. It will also up your creative confidence.

Whether using your creative gifts is new to you or you are further down that path, here's your invitation to go deeper. What began as a simple way to pass the time and challenge my heart to use my gift became an adventure filled with excitement at each corner. And all because I stayed open. Because I said yes to going somewhere new with God and I dared to try.

What awaits you on the other side of saying yes? What might be holding you back from trying? I invite you to trust God as you explore your gifts. There is something special and sacred about saying yes and walking hand in hand with God as you do. He is going to lead you into life-giving places. He will walk with you through whatever He's called you to and complete the work He's given you to do. You can trust Him to show you the markers and the breadcrumbs confirming you are on the right path. He will take you where you need to go. He's not going to abandon you even when the road gets rocky. He promises to be with you every step of the way.

your words matter.
speak LIFE.

Speak Good Things to Yourself

"YOU ARE UNIQUE."

"Jesus made each of my children unique and different shades and they are all beautiful."

"You don't have to be like anyone else, just be you."

My mom made it her mission to affirm us daily. Whether it was before we left the house for school, while she was doing our hair, or when she would catch us comparing or being critical of ourselves, she always shared some piece of encouraging wisdom.

Every weekend, my sisters and I would take turns sitting in my mom's chair to get our hair done for the week. I was always last because I was most tenderheaded. I hated getting my hair done. My hair was thick and long; it took forever, and it hurt like crazy to get it combed. If I said anything negative about my hair or compared it to one of my siblings', my mom would stop me right in my tracks and tell me how beautiful my hair was. She affirmed that each of us had different hair and it was unique to us.

She did the same when it came to the way we looked and even the shades of our skin. My skin is darker brown than some of my siblings', but we are an array of brown hues.

In a culture shaped by white supremacy and colorism, my mom was intentional about combating those messages with confident affirmations that all the different shades of melanin were beautiful. She didn't allow any room to not appreciate what we were given. We learned very early to love who we were and how we looked and wear it with pride.

Because I learned early on to marvel at and appreciate beauty, I have been able to reflect and showcase the beauty of women of color, in all of our shades of melanin and in all of our hair textures, in my art.

My father always spoke faith into me. He'd tell me exactly what he believed God could do. He'd encourage me that if I believed it, even just a little bit, I could have it. Even when I didn't know what he meant by "faith the size of a mustard seed," he'd remind me that it was enough and I could have what I believed. He instilled confidence in me so much so that to this day, I'm reminded to trust that no matter what, with a little bit of faith, "everything is gonna be alright."

With the mix of both of their words, I learned early on that there was power in what we say.

"You can do anything you put your mind to. Do it!"

My supportive parents' words gave me the confidence in adulthood to start something new, Spoonful of Faith, my art studio. I had no blueprint for this. Affirmations aren't everything, of course, but I can't overstate the impact of hearing "you can do it" and "you are creative" my entire life.

Because of this confidence, I've been able to encourage confidence in others. When a friend is low, I offer uplifting words, reminding them that they are enough and that God has a unique path for them that's soon to unfold. I've learned empathy and how to sit with them in their pain, and then hold their hand to help them stand up again. I became a safe space for them to process their feelings.

But, while I became a cheerleader for others, I had been in places in my own life where I found it hard to uplift myself.

After motherhood, life got more complicated. After I had my son, I was seriously considering not going back to work after maternity leave. *But could I pull it off?*

Sleep deprivation and the constant demands of little people made it hard to stay positive and believe that I had the time to invest in anything more. Though I was delighted in my small beginning—I was sharing my art online and started my Etsy shop, Spoonful of Faith—I had the desire to extend my reach and do more. But I was feeling like everything was stacked against me to do it. Especially my time. I didn't have hours and hours to create. I had to be a mom.

Was I making the wrong decision? Was this the right time to grow a business when I was struggling just to tend to little humans? Would it ever get easier? Often, I was overwhelmed in motherhood and not feeling like my spoonful of faith was enough.

I couldn't shake the feeling that it was the time to grow though. I wanted to lean into the spirit of my business name and have just a spoonful of faith that this could work. But I still went back and forth in my mind.

I can't do this. I don't know if I am a good enough artist to make this business work.

The only time I really had to create was during naptime or bedtime or at the end of the day when I was depleted. Early mornings were even harder for me, but on a good day, I would wake up before my kids, make my coffee, and write letters to God in my journal. It was during one of those quiet moments that I felt that I needed to let my words be a gift. I later realized it was Scripture: "Watch the way you talk. Let nothing foul or dirty come out of your mouth. Say only what helps, each word a gift" (Ephesians 4:29, MSG).

My words were meant to not only build up others but also to encourage myself in that season with young kids. I wanted to live more fully despite what I faced, and it was going to start with me and the story I was constantly telling myself. I couldn't create or share from a negative place. I needed to speak life into my own life and work.

The thought of "speaking life" stuck with and inspired me. As I drew, I began to include hand-lettered words and scriptures with my illustration pieces. At the time, there weren't many people sharing words written over their art. Lettering was a separate art form. Even though I didn't see other people mixing these two things, I knew this style was authentic to me. I had always been an encouraging voice for others, so adding life-giving words to my art felt right.

At first creating art in this new way was uncomfortable. I still struggled to believe the words I was writing. I'd find scriptures I knew God wanted me to believe but it still felt so far away. So, I tried to get around people who could uplift me.

My dad had started a weekly night at our church called Faith Clinic. Each week, he'd share a small sermon on how to have and utilize faith in our daily lives. He would encourage us to get in front of a mirror and speak God's words to ourselves. After a couple of weeks of going, I decided to try it for myself.

I spoke words of encouragement or recited scriptures to myself in my bathroom mirror. From there, I bought a pack of sticky notes and started writing words of truth and scriptures on them that I needed to believe. I stuck them on my mirror and even hid them on my desk, in my dresser drawers, and any place where I might need a reminder.

Some days I would stand in the mirror with tears because it was difficult to change the negative thoughts in my mind. Still, I kept going and with consistency, those loving words started to stick. I started to believe who God made me to be, and the path and purpose He had intended for me.

My internal narrative began to slowly change for the better. Instead of feeling defeated every day, I could no longer beat myself up about how "behind" I was. No longer did I dwell on thoughts like, *If I had just done this years ago, I'd be so much further.* I started to become the first voice to lift myself up. I became a safe place for my heart to land.

By changing the words that flowed from my mouth, I gained hope to keep going on this new journey of creativity with God. My confidence in my gift increased because the more I spoke truth to it, the more life and energy I gave it.

What words are in your heart today? Do you breathe words of life and goodness into your creativity? Or do you speak words of defeat? Maybe you haven't been an encouraging friend to yourself; you're not a loving place for yourself to land. Like me, encouraging words for others might come easily, but you may wrestle with the words in your own head.

Take a few minutes to listen and recognize what you are speaking over yourself. Sometimes we don't even notice how much of a critic we can be. As I became more aware of my thoughts and words, I started to shut my mouth or stop myself midthought with the simple word "no." This helped me to notice how often I was speaking negatively and gave me direction to stop before I spoke or let those thoughts creep in.

Find words or statements to replace those thoughts. You can find a few of them in this book. I like to use scriptures or come up with my own affirmations. The words you speak should be things that you can agree with. If it's tough for you to believe that you are the best bread baker in the world, don't say that. Maybe you start with a more loving word of life, like "I love to make _____ and God gets the glory when I use the gifts He gave me." By starting with statements that you can believe, it becomes easier to speak them over yourself.

It's normal to be in a difficult place and feel sad, discouraged, or disappointed. You do not have to pretend everything is okay as you begin to speak life. God gave us emotions and it's okay to take time to experience what you are feeling. He's big enough to hold us and be with us in those places, too. I've sat with tears and thought, *God, help me to believe these words* as I spoke truth and life to myself. Get honest with God.

I've found it helpful to incorporate affirmations into my daily routine or meditation. Like most things, you have to show up and keep showing up. If you need to write it out, write in your journal. If you need to hear it, stand in front of your mirror and speak to your reflection. Or if you would benefit most from seeing it, write sticky notes or make a memorable painting to stay encouraged. Get creative and come up with a plan that helps you keep showing up.

Remember that with work, your mind can be a safe place for you.

You will not only see your confidence grow, but it will overflow into everything you do and create. Much of our creative ability is unleashed when we align with who God says we are and what we believe about ourselves. Use your words as gifts and watch the seeds they plant grow into flourishing gardens. As you create today, speak life.

fill your minds & meditate
on things true, noble
reputable, authentic, compelling,
gracious - the best, not the worst;
the beautiful, not the ugly;
things to praise, not things to
curse.

Affirmation

I am creative.
God rejoices as I begin
to create.

Playlist

"His Words" by Grace Tena

"Brighter" by DOE

"Your Wings" by Lauren Daigle

"Be Okay" by ZOE Music

Creative Assignment

Think about how you will set the scene for creative time. Will you light a candle, play music, pray? Think about the rituals that resonate with you and help you access your creativity. List those things that will help you get started.

_____

_____

_____

_____

_____

_____

_____

_____

_____

_____

Wonder and Reflect

Look around. What fears have held you back from walking forward in your creativity?

_____

_____

_____

_____

Take a moment and think about where you're starting in your creative journey. What is your small beginning? Now close your eyes and visualize God rejoicing.

_____

_____

_____

_____

In your imagination, what does it look like for God to rejoice over you. Listen closely. What is God saying?

_____

_____

_____

_____

What three good things can you speak over yourself today?

_____

_____

_____

_____

Prayer

Lord, I come to You with my heart open in surrender. Allow my fear to release and my creativity to flow. Show me the beauty in my small and humble beginnings. I thank You for taking delight in me. Give me courage to walk forward and explore the gifts You've given me. Give me the words to speak life over who I am and what I hold. Thank You for being with me on each new adventure. Amen.

Express Yourself Here

Created
to
Shine

God uniquely formed you and shaped you in His image. Recognize the good and potential God has placed in you. Use what's in your hands and walk boldly forward in your creative calling. Your story can bring beauty into the world.

Be Who
You Were
Created to Be

WHEN I WAS in the third grade, our family moved to a northern suburb of Minneapolis. While I was used to attending a diverse school with lots of kids and teachers that looked like me and related to me, things in my new neighborhood were drastically different. I quickly realized our family was one of a few Black families in the school and the only Black family on our block. It stayed that way for most of my childhood.

My mom continued to do the work of affirming me and telling me "You are Black. You are beautiful. That's how God made you."

Still, it would take years before those words really rang true in my heart.

School can be tough; kids can be harsh. I will never forget the bright sunny summer day that my siblings and I were walking to the neighborhood park. A group of teenage boys drove by shouting racial slurs as they scowled at us. It was terrifying harassment of children. I don't like to think about it, because it still angers me and brings me to tears.

But it wasn't just the big obvious stuff like that that made it hard to exist in that space. Though I was a social child and easily made friends, I always felt like an outsider. I'd get my hair braided and have kids want to touch me like I was some foreign object. I learned to overlook and be Minnesota-nice with those who hurled microaggressions my way.

Being one of only a few Black girls in my elementary school was also hard. Even with the support of my friends, I still felt like I wasn't enough for some and too much for others. I heard that I was too loud, too talkative, too much. I kept my creativity and ideas to myself because I didn't feel that all of me was welcome. Through junior high and high school, I joined track and cheerleading and had strong friendships, but I still felt like I didn't quite fit outside of those circles. Most days I'd make myself fit into what I thought others needed me to be. I'd mask my true self to be likeable and funny, to make friends.

My friends couldn't relate to the shows we watched at home, like *Moesha* and *That's So Raven*. Sometimes it felt easier to just try and fit in and wear what everyone at my school was wearing. It was easier to laugh along when they were talking about whatever shows they had all watched and go with the crowd than to be myself.

On the first day of sixth grade at the larger middle school, I ran into a friend and old neighbor I used to jump rope with when we were six. Seeing a familiar Black girl in my grade felt like a gift from God. This school was more diverse and there was another Black girl that I knew! What could be better? We instantly reconnected and were inseparable all the way through college.

In high school and college, I found a community of friends from different backgrounds and religions and from different parts of the globe, such as Cuba, Liberia, Laos, and Dominican Republic. They welcomed me. We weren't all Black and we didn't have the same struggle, we had the same *struggles*. In those friend groups, I was able to learn about different cultures but also observe how they appreciated their deep roots in their home country. And though celebrating Black culture came easy, I acutely felt that I'd been robbed of knowing the origins and the stories of my ancestral roots.

Some things stay with you, even after you've moved on. I hadn't realized how much I had internalized the microaggressions, from being "othered," from the stares,

you are carefully crafted + wonderfully made.

from not feeling like I could be my whole self in majority-white spaces. Yes, my family and my all-Black church affirmed my identify in Christ. All my life I'd heard that I was fearfully and wonderfully made, but what did that mean, anyway? And out there, out in real-world America, why did it feel like my Blackness was an alternative from the norm instead of the intentional design of God?

It wasn't until my midtwenties on that transformative night, I would finally grasp the truth that I was made in God's image and wonderfully so. Now years later in my quiet time with the Lord, He pointed me to look at my own children. Each of them was different in their own beautiful way. He felt the same about His children, including me. I hold part of His image within me, yet I am still unique: my skin, my hair, my thoughts, my essence were thoughtfully placed just for me.

It wasn't until I heard God affirming this that it began to transform my life as well as my art. Just as in grade school, I was unsure of how I fit in the world of illustration. I hadn't realized how much the experiences in my past had kept me from confidently creating.

I started having the desire to showcase motherhood and womanhood in my art. I noticed that most of the nursery art and illustrations didn't feature women of color. You were more likely to find an image of a mother hen and her chicks than a melanated mother tenderly holding her child. So, I started drawing and sharing my own family. Then I started drawing moms and sons. People would send me their photographs and I would create drawings for them.

I wanted to continue drawing Black moms and challenged myself to #100Days OfMotherhoodSOF where I drew moms who I was connected to on Instagram.

As I consistently showed up in this way, I started gaining interest from those who had seen some of the work I shared. What I was creating was connecting to people in a genuine way. My #100DaysOfMotherhoodSOF project was noticed by *Essence* magazine. I soon had multiple inquiries for interviews and podcasts from people and platforms who wanted to know more about the girl behind Spoonful of Faith. The most common questions I got were "Why do you create the pieces you create?" and "How does the work connect to you and your story?"

Before that moment, I'd honestly never sat and thought about it. I had made what was on my heart or what I believed I was learning at the time. I was tapping into doing what authentically came from within and trying to not be influenced by everything else around me.

When I took the time to reflect and answer those questions, it hit me. All the threads of my life played a part in what I created. What was inside of my heart showed up on each of my paintings in myriad ways from florals to hand-lettering, to illustrated women and whimsical strokes.

I loved to draw women of different backgrounds and ethnicities because I struggled to see those women belong and be beloved in the world around me. My heart needed to see something different, and God's love inspired me to bring it to life. Florals signified growth and a becoming, as well as bringing a feeling of warmth, grace, and softness to what I shared. The words I used in my art were words I needed affirmed and recited over my own heart. They came from seeds planted in me from when I was that little Black girl who needed her parents' affirmations before she stepped out into the big world around her.

My unique walk and experiences were empowering me to show up to be exactly who I was created to be. And yours will, too.

Have you ever felt like you were shrinking parts of yourself to fit in? Looking back, why did you shrink away? It's so valuable to tackle this question head-on because your identity plays an important role in the journey of using your creativity. Creativity is a gift that comes from the experiences, talents, and individual characteristics you bring to the table. God desires the whole story of you, not just the parts that seem to "fit in."

Discovering this may help you heal from your past and open doors of possibility that you have never even imagined. Instead of shrinking who you are, what would happen if you asked God to guide you in using it?

I think back to some of my favorite teachers, musicians, creatives, and people in my community who I looked up to. The way they showed up, as themselves, impacted me. Many of their words and songs and much of their artwork has spoken to me in ways that only their voice could speak and reach me. I was touched because they had the courage to be who they were created to be.

God will use everything that He's placed inside of you. He'll take your experiences, your talents, and your potential and show you the good work that you've been called to do. Even if you've never been able to before, know that today, you can show up as you. If you've been broken by feeling "othered," God can redeem those experiences by giving you a new appreciation for how uniquely and intentionally He created you. Be who you were created to be.

Discovering Your Voice and Style

I HAVE SHARPENED many of my skills as a professional illustrator in drawing, sketching, and concepting ideas over the years. What used to require a lot of work, I can now quickly create without much thought. My kids love to try to get me to make things for them, and I'm always open to helping them create art and projects.

When he was six, my son, A. J., approached me with a request to draw Spider-Man. As much as I draw, that's just not something I can easily sketch. I explained this to him, but I still gave it a try because he wouldn't let me be. It looked like a superhero, but absolutely not Spider-Man.

"That doesn't look like Spider-Man!" he yelled as he grabbed the paper back.

"Well," I said, trying not to get frustrated, "that's my best right now. Maybe you can try and draw him?"

"No, I can't do it. Mine isn't good!" he huffed to me with tears welling in his eyes. I knew all too well the feeling of creating things and them not coming out like you hoped. I knew how sometimes after trying, it was hard to want to try again. I felt I had to push him toward not giving up.

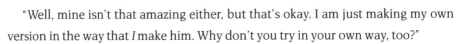

"Well, mine isn't that amazing either, but that's okay. I am just making my own version in the way that *I* make him. Why don't you try in your own way, too?"

He begrudgingly grabbed the paper back from me and stormed out the room.

"You can do it, son!" I yelled down the hallway.

He came back an hour or so later, grinning. He opened his notebook, showing me his attempts at Spider-Man and a few other characters he'd drawn. As he spoke about each one, I could sense he was proud of what he made. He was using his own creative voice, growing his own creative style. I remembered feeling that sense of pride when I was younger, too. My parents helped me grow my creative style and voice in the same way, by encouraging me to use my gifts in my own way.

Have you ever struggled with finding your creative voice? Ever had an idea and it not turn out how you saw in your mind? Frustrated with working through it, you've wanted to throw in the towel altogether? Maybe you compare everything you create to how someone else does it? You might try to emulate or copy, instead of trusting that the gift within you is just as beautiful.

When I was young, it was easy to let go, be free, and show myself loud and clear in everything. As I grew older, though, it got harder, and after I started illustrating profession-ally, it was almost impossible because I was constantly comparing myself to others. For a short season, I even began creating in another style because I thought people preferred it. I let someone else's ideas shape how I showed up creatively. The worst part was, it felt like I was wearing someone else's shoes. The style didn't fit right, no matter how hard I squeezed my toes in. My heart wasn't in the process and my true voice felt silenced.

You've been there, right? We admire well-established makers, then start to ques-tion and doubt our own abilities. Eventually, we think we need to change our way of doing things to be "better" or like them. We miss the reason that these creatives feel special to us. That they didn't arrive here overnight. They shine because they have honed their voice and distinct style over time.

Unnerved that I was losing my connection to my art, I decided to change my tactic. I began to show up in my sketchbook and let my pen flow freely, unrestrained. As I drew,

"God is leading you to create, trust your Creator."

I watched my love for different ideas and subjects spill out onto the paper: women, stories, and hope and joy. Illustrations of women covered the white space alongside encouraging words and inspiring quotes. The more I drew, the more I noticed how natural my art and style came to me. My direction became clear and my artistic voice more recognizable.

Do you struggle with putting your personal touch on things because it doesn't look or feel like those who have been doing it for years? My friend, your distinct voice and style is valuable. It has been given to you with purpose. The more you take the time to operate in it and appreciate your own voice, you will notice just how much it uniquely shines.

TRUST THE STYLE AND VOICE GOD'S GIVEN YOU

Stay focused on what is meant for you. God is leading you to create, trust your Creator. Sometimes that might look like moving in a way that not everyone else is or getting comfortable with creating differently. When it came to my unique style, I used to get comments on the way I decided to draw things. People either loved how it was different or unique, or they would question why I drew the way I did. I mentioned before that I close the eyes on the women I draw. I would often receive messages asking me why. I even had people who told me they wished I opened the eyes. It sounds silly, and not something I'd ever message someone on Instagram about, but it happened. After hearing those comments, I thought about changing my style, even though I knew I wasn't great at drawing open eyes. Part of me wanted to make people happy. But I knew I had to stick to what felt like me. Trying to change my style to please others wouldn't make me happy and wouldn't be true to myself.

As I grew artistically, I began to appreciate all the little quirks that made my work unique to me. I learned to trust what's been placed in me, where God's set me, and the distinct perspective I have been given to share. It's fine to accept criticism but make sure that you don't allow the opinions of others to throw you completely off the path or direction that God has set you on.

Here are a couple of ways to discover (or rediscover!) your voice:

Get Inspired in New Ways

When I go out for the day, I'll take photos of what inspires me. Or jot down a note about something I read that encouraged my heart. Then, when I sit down to create, I can bring those items to the table to help me think outside the box and find new ideas. Collecting inspiration from your life helps you stay more focused and connected to create more authentically. Using your personal inspiration also helps you to not be tempted to follow or copy something just because it's popular or trending.

Take on a Challenge

Keep showing up. You may not feel like you are making progress or even able to see a clear vision or style in what you create, but if you keep coming back to it faithfully, you will make progress.

As I was working through developing my style, I just kept showing up in my sketchbook. I'd throw a sketchbook in my purse so that if I found a moment of time, I could use it. You can set time in your schedule to dedicate to practicing your gifts. For instance, I would watch my sister, an amazing baker, save recipes and ideas of things she wanted to make, and then plan it into her schedule. She would consistently show up to create.

Creative challenges have also helped me be consistent. With an idea or theme, a thirty-day challenge helped me get better at making patterns, for example. This focused study helped me to create only within that theme and was helpful in developing my style. At the end of the thirty days, I was able to see my progress.

So, find a challenge that will help you show up consistently, and watch your style emerge. At the end of the challenge, you'll have created enough that you can look back and clearly see what areas need more work and where you have grown. Trust what you are learning and practicing and stay faithful in it. Over time, you'll be able to clearly communicate your ideas and expressions through your work with much less effort than when you began.

Do not be afraid to walk forward boldly as you develop your voice and style. You are beautifully made in the image of God, and as you let your individuality and voice shine brightly, you are honoring God's creation of you.

Use What You've Got

AS THE MIDDLE child of seven, I understood we couldn't afford to buy everything new. My parents weren't magic genies, waiting to grant my every wish. I was no stranger to hearing no, especially growing up with six siblings. In our home, you had to earn an allowance, show responsibility, and usually throw in some begging and pleading to make a case for anything you really wanted.

So, sharing became the way of my world. There were some perks, like getting my older, cooler sister Naya's hand-me-down clothes and not having to use my allowance to buy things I could borrow from a sibling. But when sharing wasn't an option, I got creative and used what was available.

I had always wanted my own room. I dreamed of it, a space to call mine. Unfortunately, our house combined with our big family just couldn't accommodate this dream. I knew I'd have to wait for my older sisters to vacate their rooms before I would have the chance. The waiting felt unbearable. How could I use what I had to create a space I wanted? I looked around the room I shared with my little brother, Wade.

The previous owners had used our room as a nursery. There was an accent wall with baby Mickey Mouse wallpaper that needed to go. The carpet was gray, and our big brown bunkbed set was pushed into the corner of the room. Our TV sat on the dresser, and there were a few baskets of clothes in the corner.

I could see the vision take shape: a space of my own. It was time for a bedroom makeover. I sat down and doodled ideas for things I wanted to change, furniture I wanted to move; I sketched up how I'd rearrange everything. I shared my ideas, and with a few tweaks, I got my parents and my roommate on board.

I used every square inch of that small room to create a new possibility within those four walls.

I strung lights from the ceiling, put a few shelves on the wall to showcase some of my sports awards. I hung a large mirror near the door. I couldn't move our bunk beds too much, but I put my desk in the corner, hung posters on the newly painted red accent wall, and bought a cheap bean bag chair from Walmart to fit next to the bed. I organized our books into bookcases and neatly stacked our shoes under the bunk bed. Anything that didn't have a space was hidden away in our closet.

When I was finished, the room was still far from what I had dreamed but felt like the new space I needed. My parents were proud of what I'd created and glad that I'd found a temporary solution to my problem. I spent much of my youth crafting, creating, and planning in that room. I could be proud of my little creative oasis because I made use of what I had.

Friend, my younger self embraced the beauty of creative potential and didn't shy away from using the power she already possessed to change her world—even if it was a small room revamp. You, too, can change your world with the abilities and gifts that God has given you. You've been entrusted with a set of talents, abilities, and perspectives: your own creative portion from God. Do you see the power and potential that you already have? Or are you overlooking the potential you have in your hands?

Sometimes, if I am not careful, I think I need to have more—more talent, more knowledge, more skill—to move forward with where the Lord is urging me to go. I think that more is the key, that my creative portion isn't enough. I overlook what God have given me.

When I started out, I didn't have many of the creative tools I saw other artists using. I didn't even know how to make digital illustrations, which is now a major part of the work that pays the bills. Back then, I created everything by hand. Then, I would take photos of the drawings, email the photo to myself, and edit it on my computer with a free photo-editing app. The process was super-tedious. The quality wasn't clean, crisp, and clear like the artists' I followed online. I struggled with feeling like what I had to offer was enough. I felt like if I had the professional tools, maybe I'd be a better artist.

When my kids were two and four, we would buy the cutest gifts for their birthdays and Christmas—normally something tied to their favorite TV shows and characters. We'd watch as they opened the presents, anxious to see the joy on their faces. Invariably, after a few minutes of examining the new toy, our kids would be more interested in the box or bag the item came in than the actual present.

They'd jump into the box and pretend it was a race car, or even tip it over and create a playhouse or creepy cave. I'd join in, grabbing the box cutter to make holes for windows or getting down on all fours to push them down the halls, laughing at their giggles as we swung around the corners of the house.

Turns out, my kids were on to something. Play was more fun with a blank canvas. Watching my children use their ideas and imagination brought me back to my little creative oasis, where I could use what I have. I was inspired to dig deep, run past obstacles, and use my creative portion well. If I had the desire to create something, starting with what didn't look like much, I remembered my children. I allowed the creative portion that I already possessed to shine.

You have a well-portioned dose of creativity, too. Your resources may be few, but trust the portion that God has given you is enough. See the blank canvas and embrace the lack of tools. Yep. If you are sitting there thinking of all you don't have yet, that can be a promising place. Embracing this will stretch your creative muscle and challenge you to see what can become with what you already hold.

Feeling uninspired? Allow yourself to sit in that place. Don't rush to Google or Pinterest for ideas, a blueprint, or a step-by-step DIY guide. While these things can be helpful, sometimes those influencers convince us that what we really need is to buy this tool, that gadget, or that course in order to create. Or we turn to social media for inspiration instead of pulling from our own lives, stories, experiences, and surroundings. We'll look for a picture of a pretty bouquet instead of noticing the flowers in our neighborhoods. Our easy access to any and everything online can push us further away from our natural figure-it-out mentality.

Resist the urge for more. Your real flex is the art of doing the best you can with what you have. Take a walk. Dig up old family photos. Have a conversation with an elder. Learn to rely on the creative portion you already possess.

When God called you, He qualified you for whatever the work ahead of you was, right then and there. You have everything you need to walk forward in your purpose, even if it doesn't feel that way all the time. Potential doesn't always begin with a

mapped-out plan but often stems from doing what you can now and watching it grow along the way. You can trust that God has given you everything you need to take the next step. You may want more, but instead work with your creative portion, just like I did in my childhood bedroom. See it as enough for today. As you keep using it, you will grow in skill and unlock even more of what you need along the way.

God has given you a creative portion; how will you use it?

Affirmation

I am wildly loved as my unique self.

I was divinely and beautifully made.

Playlist

"Wake Up" by Terrian

"Imagine Me" by Kirk Franklin

"Masterpiece" by Tori Kelly

"I'm Fully Known" by Tauren Wells

"No Longer Bound" by Forrest Frank and Hulvey

Creative Assignment

Find your style: Look back on things you have created. What do you like or dislike about what you've made? Can you see your style emerging? How might you describe the style you are seeing? Ask a friend or relative to look over some of your past work and share some words that help explain your style or the direction it is headed.

_____

_____

_____

_____

_____

_____

_____

_____

_____

_____

_____

Wonder and Reflect

When you create and use your gifts, how do they reflect who you are? What parts of your story are weaved through what you do?

_____

_____

_____

_____

In what ways does your voice and style show up in your life?

_____

_____

_____

_____

List the things you think you lack, things that you feel are holding you back from taking the next step in your creativity. Now, make a list of "your portion"— the tools and resources and the vision to create. How can you practice "do the best you can with what you have" this week?

_____

_____

_____

_____

_____

Prayer

Lord, thank You for the gift of my uniqueness. Allow me to see the intricate pieces You've placed inside of me and have gratitude for them. Help me to be confident in what I have to offer and the power of my story. Show me how to live out who You created me to be.

Express Yourself Here

the Posture

of Your

Heart

Using your creative gifts is a form of worship to your Creator. God can use your difficult challenges in unexpected ways to honor Him. True and honest worship comes from the heart and overflows into everything we create.

Do It as Worship

FOR YEARS, MY business had been in a growth phase, and I had developed an unhealthy cycle of creating from a place of productivity. I wanted to make what I knew would sell. I focused on wanting to please others with my artwork, and I started to feel disconnected from what I was making. My obsessions with perfection and pleasing the customer were invading my creative process and sucking the life out of my God-given giftings. Making art was no longer fun or joyful.

Most people had no idea that I was struggling. From the outside, they saw success and a full plate, but on the inside, I was a mess. I had no time or space for anything or anyone. My sole focus was building my business. I was pouring out of an empty place. Once again, I came to the end of what I could physically do. My body and mind crashed, begging for rest. I needed to recenter myself. I stopped accepting projects and closed my shop.

I had been so busy doing that I quit going to God for direction. I knew I needed to start prioritizing time with Him. When I finally sat before Him, all I could do was cry. I felt stuck creatively and was not motivated to draw or make anything. The pressure to make the perfect thing or be the best artist weighed me down. I wanted the freedom to just create because it was a God-given gift of mine. As I continued to sit with God, I could feel His peace and comfort wrap around me like a warm hug. He was there even when I had nothing to offer but tears.

I committed to quiet times with God, moments of pause to find my direction. After a few weeks, I was finally ready to try to create. I sat at my desk, my watercolor paper in front of me and all my art tools surrounding the page. I wasn't sure what to create. I knew I didn't want to end up in the same place as before, worrying about making the perfect piece of art, but where would I start? Then, I clearly heard these words in my heart: *Do it as worship, daughter.*

Do it as worship? It was a new phrase, but I immediately connected with it. God was telling me to just show up and create as worship. *Was that even possible?* What would worshipping with my creativity even look like? I sat and pondered the idea for a minute. I wanted to try. The more I started saying the phrase, the more excited I got about the possibility. In that very moment, a burden I had held for so long was released. If simply accepting in my heart to give it a try felt this good, how would things change when I started to use my creativity as an offering of worship?

Turns out, creating as an act of worship would transform everything. Just like I had done in my quiet time with God, I set up my creative time with intention. I made my coffee or tea, turned on my light, took out all the art tools I wanted to use, and turned on music—sometimes worship music, sometimes a mix of various genres. Then, I focused my heart on receiving from God, just like I did anytime I had prayed or sang in worship. I set my heart and mind on His goodness and each time, the pressure would fall off and the creativity flowed. As I created as worship, I honored God with the gift He gave me.

Instead of worrying about the outcome, I simply showed up and worshipped. I talked to God and asked for ideas. Sometimes the ideas came quickly and other times nothing would spark. So, I would doodle or paint while I waited and worshipped. Often, by just creating, an idea would come to mind. Whatever God wanted to come out of this time, I was open. And it didn't have to be painting or drawing; I kept my heart open to however He wanted to use the creativity within me. Sometimes I'd make things for my kids or I'd write up ideas for future projects. Through the process, I'd trust that if I worshiped Him with my creativity, then He'd lead me to the ideas.

Speak good
things
to yourself.

After every session, peace would come over my heart from the time we spent together. Finally, after all those years of striving for perfection, I had found my way out of the toxic cycle. Through worship, I had freedom to create from my heart and to glorify God with my gifts. Instead of pressure, I felt confidence and joy as I created in that sacred place. Anytime I found myself starting to get stuck again, I'd lay all my worries back down and make time to recenter through worship.

During one of these daily practices, I made a breakthrough. The flow, the connection that I'd longed for, poured out of my soul. I was determined not to stop until the flow stopped. It had been so long since I'd been in the creative zone. I wasn't sure how it would turn out, but I felt moved and inspired and even surprised at what was appearing on the watercolor paper.

Do it as worship.

The thought kept echoing in my mind.

Do it as worship.

I was finally climbing out of the rut I had been trapped in.

When I stepped back from my page, I had illustrated a group of women hidden behind colorful flowers and florals. Their faces were drawn in black lines, almost covered by the flowers, but still visible. Each woman was beautifully blending in and had also been found. She was not lost anymore. I saw echoes of my own story in the art.

I had been one of those women, lost in my worries, my control, my plans. I had been stuck in a negative spiral and God was pulling me out. I was found. It was an overwhelming moment of clarity, a meaningful piece of art, born out of sincere worship.

Have you ever felt the weight of feeling lost? Lost in your worries, your thoughts, unsure of what is up or down? Empty from your doing? On the other end, have you ever experienced the joy and awakening in being found? Remembered, affirmed, and sure, standing on solid ground? When you worship God with your creativity, you will gain affirmation, assurance, and grounding. Worship awakens your creativity and gives you a joy unlike anything else.

Friend, there is freedom in worship. What would it look like to worship God with your gifts? How could you set aside the time to think on Him, to honor Him, as you create? Worship does not just have to be in song, dance, or creativity. As you go about your life, weave worship throughout your day. Your nurturing, your teaching, your cleaning, your organizing, your hospitality can all be used to worship. When you think of everything you do as doing it for God, every act, every move, every thought becomes a way to honor Him. God gets the glory in it all. Worshipping will transform your heart to focus on God and the beauty of His gifts within you. Your heart will align to His and allow your gifts to flow freely. Just as we worship in song and lift our voice, we can lift our paintbrushes (or whatever tool you use to create) and make in joyful worship to Him.

Take the time to make space in your life to praise Him. Adding another thing to your day or fitting it in with a schedule that already feels tight might feel difficult, but the results are incalculable. Spend a few moments in the shower or as you get ready for your day to think of where you can weave in creative time with God. Create margin to sit, dream, and make with the Creator. Maybe it's after the kids are in bed or early morning before they are awake. Or maybe you'll find margin during a lunch break at work. Make time to meditate and dwell on His goodness in your life as you use your gifts.

When you spend intentional time worshipping God with your gifts, you lean into the truth that God has formed you and knows you. He will shower you with love and remind you that you are not lost. God is still there, still at work in your life. So, create, write, and make for His glory. Offer your gifts in dedicated worship. Be fully present in His presence and receive His inspiration. I promise, you will be stunned at what comes through on the other side of your joyful worship. You are found in your beautiful Creator.

In Spite Of

WHAT'S WRONG WITH ME?

I lay on the sunken-in living room couch at our house. It was the end of senior year, and this was supposed to be an exciting time but instead I had been hit with some sort of illness. I'd woken up days earlier feeling drained and exhausted. Like I had ran a marathon that no one told me about. When I'd walk or get up, my leg and arm joints felt worn and achy. I wasn't eating much, had trouble keeping anything down, and had a slight fever. My family and I suspected I had the flu. Whatever it was seemed to knock the wind right out of me. As the days went by, I wasn't getting better. After about a week, my oldest sister, Nisha, volunteered to take me to the doctor just to make sure I was okay.

We headed to the local urgent care down the road from our house. Feeling so helpless, I struggled to sit comfortably in the waiting room chairs. I felt more nauseated by the moment. When our names were called, they ushered me into a room and rushed to get me fluids. The nurse asked me questions that I half answered. I lay on the cold hospital bed with not much energy or care. My sister stepped in as my advocate and made sure I shared all the details. I could feel the cold rush of the fluids through my veins—they were helping. The doctor ordered a few blood tests and we waited. I was nervous. When the doctor came back in, she said something didn't seem right. She wanted us to go to the ER instead. I worried. *Maybe this isn't the flu?* But that was as far as my thoughts ran. I was so fatigued. I didn't have the energy to think.

When we made it to the hospital, the tests continued. I was assigned a room and told I'd be kept overnight. One night turned into fourteen stressful days with few answers. I had seen almost every doctor in the place. I felt like a case study and a test animal. I gave blood every day and was wheeled around to X-rays and MRIs to see what was going on with me. My family would come and spend time with me, but I was miserable. Exhausted. And I let everyone know it. I just wanted to go home.

"We're going to run more tests."

I stayed in the raised hospital bed, glaring at the doctor. *More tests? Why can't they just figure this out and help me feel better?* No one had answers, only more questions. I was sick of lying in the hospital bed, waiting for answers. No one could tell me why I was still sick. They believed it might be an autoimmune disease, but the only way they could tell which disease was by ruling out others. This meant I had to endure another round of blood tests, MRIs, CT scans, and more. *When would this end?*

Eventually, the doctor would utter a diagnosis that changed my life. "You have lupus."

What? I briefly recalled a friend of the family with the same diagnosis, but it still felt hard to wrap my mind around what this meant for me.

"It's a chronic disease that you'll have to manage for the rest of your life."

I blacked out. I can't remember how the conversation went after that. My face had likely frozen from shock. I didn't fully understand the weight of what they were saying; the medical terms went in one ear and out the other. I would find out later that lupus is an autoimmune disease that involved my immune system attacking its own tissues. It can affect the joints, skin, blood cells, and even more serious organs like the kidneys, heart, and lungs. I was shocked. I was upset.

Sitting with the weight of a lupus diagnosis at nineteen was a lot to handle. I had begun to feel physically better and more like myself again, but I was frustrated with the diagnosis. I wasn't sure how it would impact my future, but I also felt a sense of relief. We figured out what was causing my symptoms. I could finally go home.

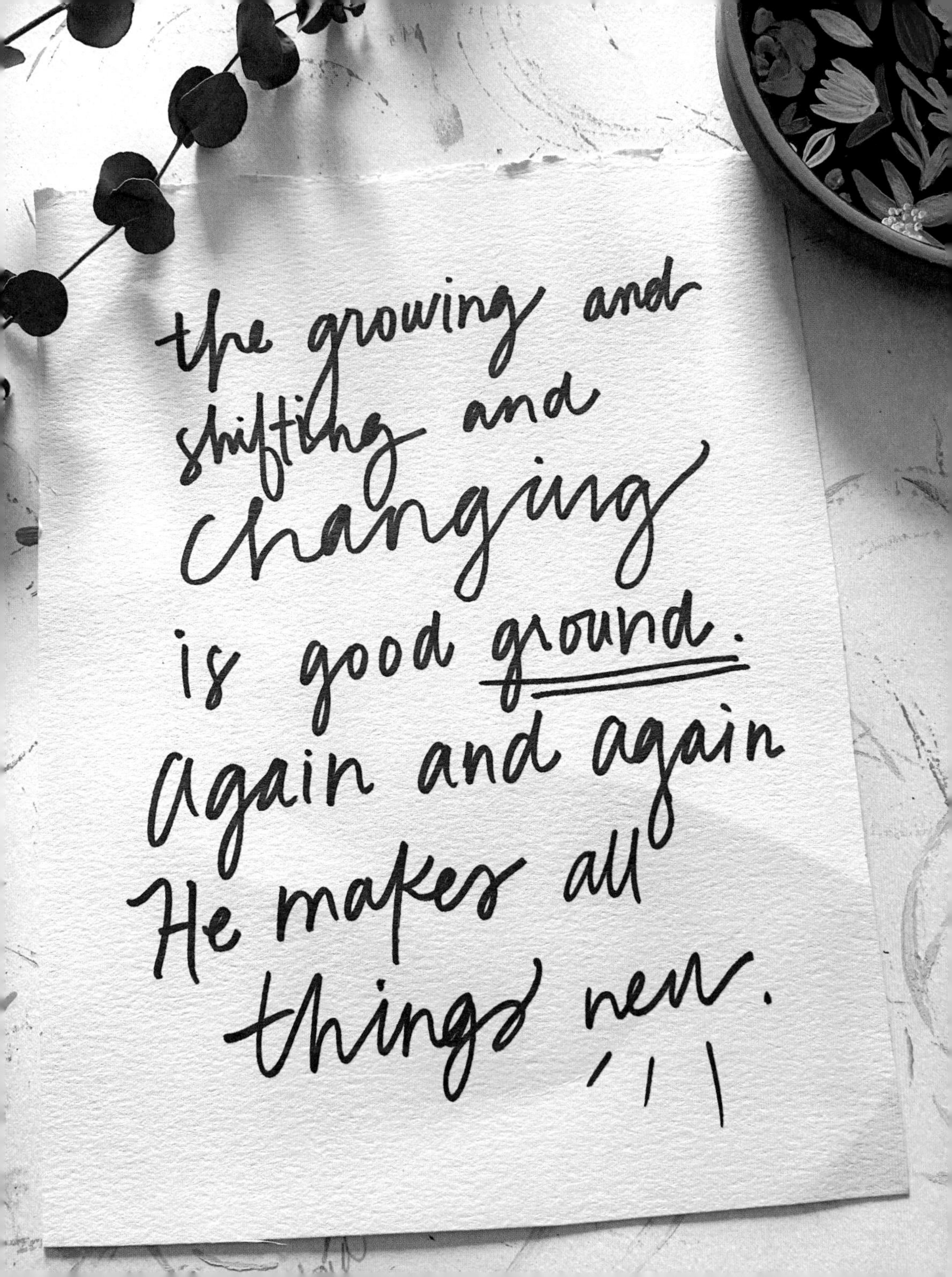

the growing and
shifting and
changing
is good ground.
again and again
He makes all
things new.
' / |

"I didn't know how to move forward, but I knew it was time to get back up."

" I know how to get along and live humbly, and I also know how to enjoy abundance and live in prosperity. In any and every circumstance I have learned the secret, whether well-fed or going hungry, whether having an abundance or being in need.

I CAN DO ALL things through Christ who strengthens me. "

Philippians 4:12-13 (AMP)

trust in the Lord with all your heart.

After two terrible weeks of testing and confinement in a hospital bed, I was sent home with a referral to find a rheumatologist—and a plethora of thoughts, emotions, and questions to wrestle with for myself and with my new doctor.

If you've lived long enough, you've been through something that has knocked the wind out of you. You may have wondered if life would ever be the same or how your future would be impacted. Life-altering diagnoses, severe accidents, and natural disasters change your life in an instant.

Lupus would affect me, to various degrees, for the rest of my life. I often wondered whether I would have the energy to raise a family, run a business, or even live life. In a particularly tough season where I was feeling defeated, I had watched a story on the news about a woman, Amy Palmiero-Winters, who is an amputee. Over her life, she had experienced tragedy and many obstacles, but she had a dream to run marathons. As an adult, she finally accomplished that dream and holds many national awards and titles. As I listened to her story, I thought of how she could have sulked in her inability to run like everyone else. She could have let the physical and emotional pain of learning a new skill stop her. But she didn't. This woman kept getting back up and fighting for the goal she believed she could reach.

Choose to live, I thought. I felt God encouraging me, urging me to live the best life I could in spite of my diagnosis. I didn't know how to move forward, but I knew it was time to get back up. I was not alone in my struggle, and I was not the only one struggling. I thought, *Everyone is going through something, and I want to help others who needed that push like I did to keep going.*

I made myself available to do anything that helped others. I'd hear of a friend who was going through a difficult time, and I'd reach out to pray for them. I'd ask God to put people on my heart so I could create artwork as a gift of encouragement. When it came to work, I would sit longer until I felt a clear direction of what to focus my energy on next. I desired to use my creativity in a way that would allow every part of my life to shine for God's glory.

As I drew, I prayed over the pieces, "Lord, may this art bless any who sees it." I prayed over the T-shirts I made, "God, may each shirt be a reminder of Your love to any who wear it. May they actually feel Your love." I wasn't sure what might happen, but I prayed furiously, intentionally, over everything, and in spite of the pain I had experienced within my own body.

What happened next blew me away. I started to receive responses from women who were impacted by the images and artwork I had created. They felt connected and affirmed in their identity by the illustrations. I didn't realize all the ways God could use the power of creativity to bring healing. I didn't know He could use art to penetrate hearts and show these women that they were uniquely created and loved by their Creator. I didn't know it could all come through a paintbrush.

What difficult seasons or circumstances have you faced in life? Did the trials seem to push you off track or feel like an unmovable obstacle? Friend, those circumstances do not need to derail your creativity. As you walk your own path, you can create in spite of and through the hard moments of life. God can redeem your circumstances. He can use your gifts to bring healing to yourself and those around you.

God has given you a gift, and He delights in your learning to use it well, through the plentiful seasons and through the tough seasons. Allow the journey through difficult seasons to push you toward deeper and more meaningful work. Ask God to use everything in your life—the good and the hard—to bring new meaning to your creative pursuits and deepen your heart to use this gift to bless your life and others. When you do, you'll discover an increase in your empathy and capacity to love others better.

hope

From
the Heart

IT WAS A powerful dream. There were two groups of people worshipping and glorifying God. The first group worshipped in the exact same way—almost robotic. They all stood in a line doing the same move over and over with their hands. They looked to be performing instead of worshipping freely.

The second group worshipped with abandon. Some sang, some cried, some danced, some spoke in foreign tongues. Even in a dreamlike state, I could sense the sincerity in their hearts.

When I awoke, I had tears in my eyes. I didn't understand fully, but that dream had touched me. As I sat there in my bed, I began to connect the dots of what I had dreamed. I knew the dream was showing me that true and honest worship comes from the heart.

I couldn't shake the idea for months. I'd spend quiet time thinking about the dream and asking God to help me become more sincere in everything I did. During my quiet time, I read Ephesians 2:10, which reminded me that we are God's handiwork and created for good works. While studying the passage more, I learned that the word *handiwork* comes from the Greek word *poiema*, which translates to "something made." *Poiema* is also the root of the English words *poem* and *poetry*. I sat and thought of us each being a piece of the poetry that God made, each person a unique word, adding something different to build a beautiful poem.

The diversity and beauty found within worship has shaped pivotal moments throughout my creative journey. Just like God loves creativity in our backgrounds and cultures, He loves to see His people use the diverse creative talents He's given. I realized, just like the people in my dream, when I was sincere and honest about the gifts God gave me creatively, there was incredible freedom. I realized just how special my art and creativity were to God. So special that He intentionally put them in me.

All creation speaks to God's artistry. Our sincere worship is the evidence of our devotion to our Creator. It stems from our love and gratitude. Most importantly, adoration and the way in which we reflect God looks different in each of us.

God loves to work in different ways in different people. When we honor the way in which we were created and sincerely show that in what we do or make, we get a chance to reflect the diversity of who God is. Having a heart to glorify Him through our creativity allows us to authentically show up as ourselves in sincere worship.

"We get a chance to reflect the diversity of who God is."

its all worthy
of worship.

Today, as you create:

GIVE THANKS

When we worship and glorify through song or prayer, we often use praise and thanksgiving with our words and in our hearts to glorify God. So, what does it look like to apply the same idea to our creative gifts? What happens when we move, make, and create with that same posture? In our thanksgiving for the gift and ability to use it, we give Him glory.

STAY HUMBLE

Don't let any of that divine goodness go to your head—because it's God's goodness shining through, anyway. Stay humble and depend on Him to direct you in using your gift. Encompass His heart of love and grace as you practice, gain skill, and share the creative gifts with others.

PRAY

Not one of us will express God's glory the same way. So, as we honor Him in our creative gifts, ask Him in prayer how He desires you to do it. Be open to the response and the unique ways in which God gave you to honor and glorify Him with what has been placed within you.

Affirmation

In spite of my circumstances, I was created to worship.

Playlist

"Psalm 42" by Tori Kelly

"Grace" by Bri Babineaux

"When I Pray" by DOE

"First and Only" by Elevation Worship

"Loving Kind" by Antoine Bradford

Creative Assignment

Set up a creative session with a focus on just creating as a way to honor and worship God this week. Do your best to release the expectations of what will take place. Set up time to draw, write, mold, or create in whatever way you do. Write about your experience.

_____

_____

_____

_____

_____

_____

_____

_____

_____

_____

Wonder and Reflect

How do you envision your creative process changing when you decide to worship by using your gift?

_____

_____

_____

_____

Have you ever wanted to quit because of challenging circumstances in your life? How did you choose to live your best life despite difficult times?

_____

_____

_____

_____

Reflect on a hard period in your life. How did that trial impact the way you used your creative gifts? What did creativity look like? How did it feel?

_____

_____

_____

_____

_____

_____

_____

Prayer

Lord, thank You for the gift of creativity. Illuminate the giftings and creativity that I have within. As I use my creativity, please help me to release my expectation and do it as worship. Show me how to embrace the freedom that creating in this way offers to my life. I appreciate and want to honor You with my creations.

Express Yourself Here

Grow at Your Own Pace

God honors the creative roots you are planting and growing beneath the surface. Much of your hard work won't be seen right away, but you are sure to see good and steady growth over time. Grow at your own pace, and remember to celebrate the small steps.

Honor the Journey

I STARTED MY first business with my older sister and younger brother when we were in elementary and middle school. It wasn't legally formed, just a couple of kids who saw a need in the neighborhood and wanted to do something about it. It wasn't a noble need either, unless you consider chocolate bars and bags of potato chips helping mankind. We'd bike a couple miles to the nearest gas station in our city and come back with snacks and candy to sell to kids on our block. We called it the "snack shack." We didn't make much money, we just added a couple quarters to each item and split the profits to add to our piggy banks. And that wasn't the only business idea we would try.

One summer we were bored, so we invited everyone on the block to come and hang out in the garage while my parents were at work. We charged a dollar to get in. We set up games with prizes for the neighborhood kids to play, sort of like a mini carnival. It was totally unsupervised and secretly hidden from the adults. We eventually did get caught and we got in trouble from my parents, but I know they admired the fact that we even pulled it off in the first place.

As a seasoned creative entrepreneur, looking back, I see there were always threads throughout my life leading to what God had already planned and promised over me. Even when I didn't notice, the threads—the entrepreneur, the innovator, the community connector—had always been there.

Can you look back over your years and see it, too? Maybe you were always hanging on the words in the pages of books and the love of language and writing has always been within. You might have been the visionary, the planner, the one all your friends ran to for ideas of something fresh to imagine. Maybe you were the kid who was getting messy, knee-deep in dirt making forts and sandcastles; you loved constructing and building. Whatever the case, even if we never noticed until now, the promises and purposes God made us for can often be seen divinely threaded throughout our lives.

I always knew I was going to own a business. From the days of sidewalk lemonade and candy stands when I was a kid to when I'd sell my doodles that I drew during church to members after service for twenty-five cents. Two years after that morning when I sat in the rocker in my daughter's nursery, that day seemed to arrive. God impressed on my heart to start sharing my art online. I had started Spoonful of Faith while still working my corporate job. And even though at that point it was making some extra fun money, I felt a nudge to take it further than Etsy.

"I think I'm gonna do it." I took a deep breath. I was sitting across from my sister-in-law, Aisha, at a corner table at our favorite coffee shop. We'd meet often to talk, go for walks, or grab a coffee in the middle of the day, enjoying breaks from our corporate jobs.

We'd been having this conversation for a while, but on this day, things felt different and something in me was changing. "I think I am going to try to do Spoonful of Faith full-time." I was feeling a push or a wind, if you will, to go further with it. At the time, I was still pregnant with my son, A. J., and about to go on maternity leave. It felt crazy to feel this way or to be thinking of launching myself into creativity with no real safety net. "I *know* you can do it," she said. I knew it, too. I felt the same love and support from my younger sister Loryn and my mom when I told them. I didn't have a clue how or even if things would pan out, but I knew that I wanted to take a chance on this whole illustration thing.

if God gives such
attention to
wild flowers,
most of them never seen,
don't you think
He'll attend to you,
take pride in you,
do His best
for you?

LUKE 12:28

Starting a business is not for the faint of heart and it's not a dream for everyone to run after. My message is not to quit your job. My story is not going to be everyone's story and it's not supposed to be. Using your gifts doesn't mean you need to build a brand or become a small-business owner. But for me, I knew it was time to see how far it could go if I gave it my all.

Yet, how would I convince my husband? I am the dreamer. I am the girl who is filled with faith to do the risky things. He, on the other hand, thinks more logically and likes a good plan. You might have someone like this in your life. Someone who keeps you grounded or pushes you to think through all the details. I'd be lying if I didn't say that his practical mind has saved me many times.

"I can always go back to work," I said as I eased into our conversation. I was heading into maternity leave anyway, and so I'd be off work for a few months. I didn't want to go back, but I promised him I would if I had to.

"Hmm . . . I don't know," he said with reluctance. "Let's just see how things go when you're on leave and go from there."

That's all I needed to hear.

I would spend the next couple months learning how to be a mom of two and fervently searching for freelance work—determined to keep this plan going.

As each month passed, I'd get just enough work to convince my husband that it wasn't yet time to go back to my 9 to 5. It felt like two years of manna, having just enough for our daily needs. We didn't have excess funds to do fun things like date nights and weekend getaways. We were home a lot with small children. Every last dime had to be budgeted, and there were times when there wasn't enough and we had to juggle, rework, and move things around.

"You *could* go back to work," my frustrated husband would remind me.

I knew that was a possibility and maybe even the one that, on the outside, made "more sense." But faith comes easy for me. I am willing to hold out because I truly trust what God has for me. I believe in sacrificing the comfort of today for the possibility of what could be tomorrow. I could feel it in my bones and had a peace that this journey was going to end well. Besides, I hadn't been happy with the job I'd left, using my skills and time to profit a corporation. The possibilities for fulfillment in using my creative gifts to own and operate a profitable small business gave me something to look forward to. Using my gifts to help support my family was a dream and I was willing to do whatever it took to go after it.

Nevertheless, this entrepreneur life was not what I'd envisioned when I quit my corporate job. I was hustling, waking up each day ready to run after what I envisioned as success. I wanted clients, cash flow, recognition, and a business that was thriving. I'd see posts on social media praising those who were #TeamNoSleep and reminding us that we have the same amount of hours in a day as Beyoncé, so you had better get to it. I was constantly feeling like everyone around me was in grind mode, and I was influenced, believing I had to keep up this pace. And I did, but I was depending on my skills and hustle.

What came naturally as a kid felt like so much more work as I got older. Although God gave me a promise to walk with me, teach me, and guide me, I still found myself worried about how it was all going to play out. I wanted my business to grow, my skills to increase, the impact of my art to be felt, and I wanted to see progress now. When things were not panning out as quickly as the perfectly executed vision I'd imagined in my head, it felt hard to trust what God said. I questioned if He was taking me the right way. I cried and fussed and fought tooth and nail when things didn't go according to my plan. If God could do anything, then why wasn't He showing up for me like I wanted Him to?

Have you ever sat in that place before? Maybe you feel like God keeps nudging you to step forward, and when you do, things look nothing like you hoped. Maybe your heart feels hopeless or weary in your waiting. Or, like me, you are fighting for His promises in your own strength, trying to make it happen like you imagined. It can be difficult to trust in the waiting.

It was in one of those seasons that this verse encouraged me in a new way: "Hope deferred makes the heart sick, but a longing fulfilled is a tree of life" (Proverbs 13:12, NIV).

As I read it, I felt seen. Maybe because I had grown weary of being heartsick. Maybe because the verse wasn't telling me to shape up but expressing what I had known to be true, deep down. Waiting on God's promises can be tough on the heart.

While my situation didn't change right then, this felt like a reminder. God hadn't forgotten His promise or purpose for me. He knew the weariness in my heart and the depth of how it made me feel. I rushed to find my watercolor sketchbook. I needed to keep these words close. As I picked up my art tools and drew out the scripture, I found myself drawing flowers all around those words and hanging the page on the wall above my desk.

Each day following, I began the process of slowly unclenching my grip on my own plans and starting to trust God's promises. I would read that scripture and remind my heart that although the waiting was hard, one day I would see growth. I imagined a bountiful garden when I thought of my longing finally fulfilled. I encouraged myself by remembering the threads of my life that pointed to my now.

God's plan had always been at work, even if I hadn't noticed. While it didn't get easier overnight, I began to honor the journey. I started to see the important work that was being done in the process. I was learning consistency, how to build skill, how to hold on and trust His plan. My mindset started to shift and projects even began to trickle in. Like daily bread, I continued to get just enough each day to keep going. My confidence also began to increase.

We might not realize it at the time, but major work takes place in our hearts as we lean in and trust God. Our hearts begin to align with the promises He's already spoken over us from the beginning of time. God views our lives from a 360-degree perspective, seeing the full picture while we are limited to seeing what is right in front of us. He's carefully threaded His divine purpose through each of our days. So, even when we can't see it or don't understand, we can look back and trust His resume.

"Major work takes place in our hearts as we lean in and trust God."

My friend, God is thoughtful with every detail of your story. His ways are above what we plan or can even fathom. He sees you and knows you and what you're walking through. He's placed threads throughout your life that show His goodness. You can trust Him. You can trust that the gifts and creativity He placed in you will come forth in its proper time. As you hold close to Him, begin to release your expectations of how things should come to fruition. Look for the threads. Keep your heart open and don't miss what God is doing behind the scenes. When your reality does not align with what you expect, you can still trust that God's Word never comes back empty-handed.

You might find yourself in a season of waiting on God's promises. Maybe things are not going as you hoped, and you are finding it hard to hold on. All that you encounter through the waiting will not be wasted; it all works together for your good (Romans 8:28). I want to remind you that God knows the full picture and plan of your life.

Can you look back over your life and see His hand and faithfulness? Make a list of times you recall seeing God's faithfulness—those are God's fingerprints. This is His resume. Trust that God has been up to more behind the scenes than you have knowledge of. Even if you can't see His hand in your current situation, trust His resume. Sometimes this spoonful of faith is all you need to keep believing that God's promises will come right on time.

Release your expectations. Sometimes our expectations can cause us to struggle in trusting Him and cloud our judgment. If God is omniscient, as our guide and GPS, we can trust that the route He has mapped out is thoughtfully designed to get us where we need to be safely and at our appointed time. Letting go of our personal ideas and plans and clinging to the Creator's opens us up to walk forward in a path that considers the full picture.

An invitation from the Lord does not always guarantee the simplest of roads, but you never have to doubt God's faithfulness. While on the course, it is up to us to keep an open heart as we follow Him, even when it is a different route than what we have in mind. Honor the journey.

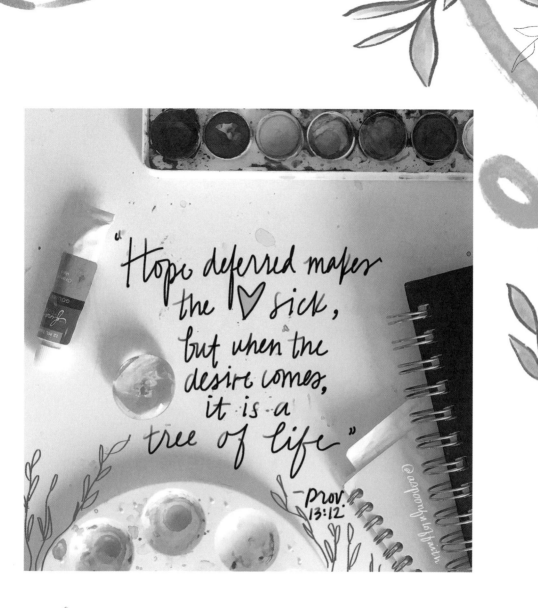

"Hope deferred makes the ♡ sick, but when the desire comes, it is a tree of life"

—Prov. 13:12

@aspoonfuloffaith

Celebrate Every Victory

A YEAR AFTER turning Spoonful of Faith into a full-time business, I was still exhausted. I was walking out this beautiful promise and creative gift, but I had quickly turned it into a mountain of work. I wasn't enjoying my life, I wasn't enjoying my family, and frankly I wasn't enjoying my attitude. I thought that the more I accomplished with my creativity and work, the happier I would be. So, I worked harder, accomplished more, and felt worse. I had fallen into a toxic spiral.

I would chase after a job with enthusiasm, land it, then immediately look for the next thing. I wasn't pausing to enjoy the win. I was too exhausted to see any of the riches around me: my beautiful family, a wonderful village of support, salvation, health, creative vision, and so much more. I had so much around me but felt nothing.

Do you know the feeling of that chase? Ever felt caught in that toxic spiral? Maybe you've felt overwhelmed by the busyness in your life. Drained by your responsibilities to your work, life, or family? Feeling like you can't stop or you'll miss something? Maybe you feel like you don't have the tools to juggle everything. Or like each ball you're trying to juggle falls as soon as it touches your hands. I've been there, friend. I've been beaten up by my expectations, blinded by success, and crushed by the demand.

There's a way out of that vicious cycle. There's a light at the end of this tunnel, and it doesn't have to lead to the death of your creativity. Instead, hope and light will give you a path to move forward with confidence.

It was a simple Instagram video that opened a door for me to step away from the nonstop and exhausting feelings. I was journaling one day on the little Ikea desk in the corner of our bedroom. As I wrote about my week, I remembered the video. Amy Hale, a woman I was following, shared about her daily journal and study practices. In the video, she mentioned a gratitude journal and how she recorded her thoughts daily. Each gratitude entry was numbered, and she was close to recording a thousand daily moments at the time. I found it so inspiring and knew I wanted to implement that into my life immediately. I wondered how many moments I was missing in my day. What would my life look like if I tracked gratitude?

It also reminded me of my dad's wisdom of the importance of writing things down. If God gave you a promise or showed you a dream or a confirming word from a friend, you'd better write it down. After all, if you didn't, then you'd likely forget and miss its impact. People forget. I've forgotten what I've eaten for breakfast! But when I took the time to write things down, I had a space to go back and remember them and be encouraged again. I could hold on to those words long after they were given to me.

Do you know there is power in writing things down? You gain more clarity, focus, and motivation when you put pen to paper. There are numerous studies that show how writing things down can help with memory and brain activity. Do you ever take the time to jot down what you're thankful for?

Taking a page from my dad's advice and inspiration from the video, I decided to make my own gratitude journal and put it to the test in my own life. I took out my paints and spent a few minutes painting a set of flowers and the word *thankful* across the cover over an extra notebook I had with my art supplies.

I was in such a busy season, so I started with a baby step, challenging myself to write in my journal daily for one month. There were no stipulations on what I needed to include or how many things I wanted to list in a day. It could be any monumental or minuscule thing. Some days it would be as small as enjoying a cup of coffee while it was still hot, or catching up with a friend, or having the opportunity to draw something in my sketchbook uninterrupted. Even if I missed a few days, it didn't matter. The point was to just keep showing up and documenting my gratitude.

I found the smaller the things I wrote about, the more meaningful the mundane days became. Like the way the sun would shine through the bedroom in the morning and hit the cheek of my toddler still at sleep. Or the twenty minutes I'd gotten that day to encourage a friend in need of comfort. Or how I'd found that paint tube that I'd been searching for weeks for, still closed, thank goodness, hidden under the couch. Every tiny win began to add to my life. If I took the time to look, I could find gratitude and joy in my everyday life. The more I counted, the more I saw how many beautiful things were taking place every day.

That journal began to inspire my creativity. When I needed inspiration for what to draw, I could pull ideas from the journal. When I needed motivation to keep going, I could look back on all the things I wrote about. It was a play-by-play of every tiny win happening in my world. Fueled constantly with joy, I watched as that joy overflowed into everything I created and made. As I'd sit down to paint or draw, I found more meaning and appreciation in what I was making. I felt more present in the process. Whatever came from the creative time, I trusted that God would make good. That not only inspired me to connect with my work but also increased the confidence I had in using my creative gifts.

At the end of the month, I dedicated time to look at old journal entries and remember where I had been. It brought tears to my eyes to see how gratitude was changing me from the inside. God's goodness was present in even the smallest of ways when I took the time to look. It was shifting my heart and my perspective on what was truly important in life. Instead of focusing on accomplishing more, the demands of work, or getting to the next thing, I was learning to appreciate the journey and count goodness all along the way. There were so many things I was able to cherish from that month. The journal was a transformative tool that helped to remind me that when I took the time to look, there was much to be grateful for.

Celebrate every Victory

ALL4FAITH

"Gratitude gives us pause and honors remembrance."

Maybe like me you've found yourself in a toxic cycle that is leaving you overwhelmed and exhausted. Maybe you've invested all your time in trying to hold all the pieces of life, and you've lost the hope and passion for what is in your hands. But when you set your heart on making room for gratitude, you will start to see how God's love and plan flow through every detail of your life. Gratitude gives us pause and honors remembrance. It brings fuel to inspire your days, increases passion for all you do, and helps to motivate

your heart toward what's truly important. When we recognize all the gifts God has given us, we can create with confidence.

I was well into my daily routine of writing in my gratitude journal when an idea dropped into my heart one morning. It was simple, really, but it was to celebrate every victory. I realized every win, every mercy or moment of favor I felt in my life was an opportunity to celebrate. Can you imagine it? Right there, where you feel no one cares or that your win seems too small, you can choose to make it a big deal and rejoice in that place. How might that inspire your confidence?

If you're like me, you've spent way too much time downplaying things you should be rejoicing. Take the time to make any small win into a moment of celebration. The celebration could be as extravagant or intimate as you want it to be. Sometimes for me it would just be a moment of prayer or thanks by myself; sometimes I'd share with friends and family, cook a fun meal, or even take a moment to scream and dance! It doesn't have to be glamorous, but it is important for us to pause and give thanks.

Take a moment to stop, reflect, and celebrate. It is up to us to not lose the moment by looking for the next. We have the power to use this as a time to be grateful for everything that is happening in our life and rejoice in it. Big or small.

> I'm thanking you, GOD, from a full heart,
> I'm writing the book on your wonders.
> I'm whistling, laughing, and jumping for joy;
> I'm singing your song, High God.
>
> Psalm 9:1 (MSG)

If you are feeling like you don't have much to rejoice over, I challenge you to walk in gratitude. Maybe like my story, you're running from one thing to the next and not taking time to pause. You might be losing hope in why you started in the first place. Take a moment to start counting the good. Look for the little things and put your focus back on the Creator and all He has already placed before you. Celebrating and being grateful can be a saving grace in a trying season. While I was waiting on things to grow and see the promises God had given me in my creative journey, God was showing me that I already had much to behold. You do too, friend.

I encourage you to pause and rejoice over every little piece of your beautiful, creative life. Let it inspire you to cherish what is in your hands. Remind your heart not to overlook any of it. Not one single thing. You'll be overwhelmed at the joy you will find and the hope it will give you to push forward confidently in all God has for you ahead.

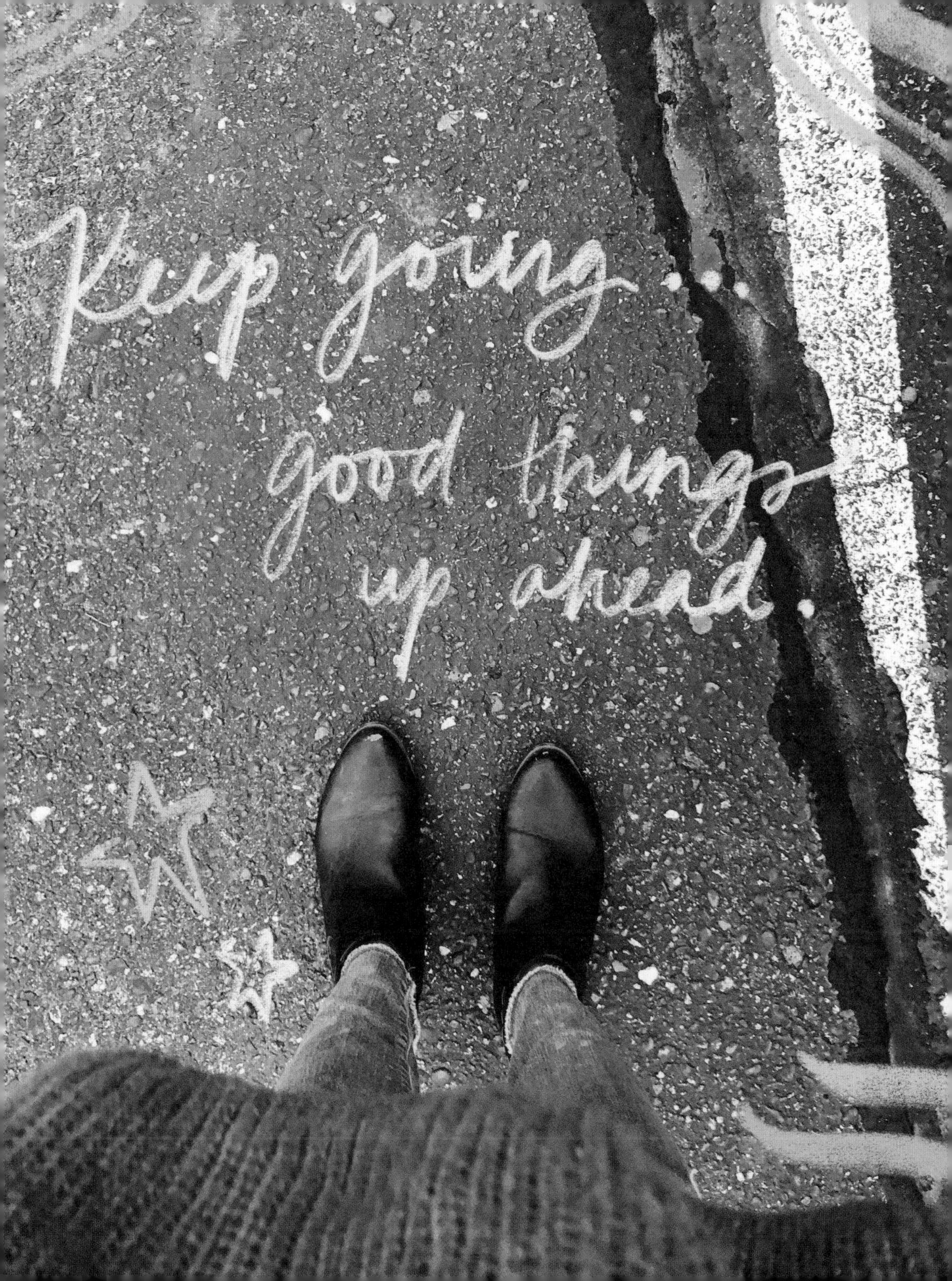
Keep going...
good things
up ahead.

Create
to Create

HAVE YOU FOUND yourself asking these questions?

I am finding success, but is this something I can keep up with?
I feel like I'm drowning; is it just going to feel this way for a season?
How could I do this for the long run?
Can God use things like art and creativity for His glory? Is it enough? Is it useful? How can something like my illustrations be used for His glory? Do I have to make sure I post them online? Plan to sell them?

Have you ever struggled with believing the gifts you have are useful? Maybe they do not look big or glamorous. You may know God's given you the heart to use them, but you don't think what you create will mean anything or bring value. You might believe it won't make a difference if you use it or not.

But sometimes you just need to stop.

Whenever I start having doubts and asking questions like this, I know it's time to pause. These thoughts reveal that I've lost sight of the joy and freedom available to me as I pursue creativity. This is when I know it's time to free myself to create for the sake of creating. To stop and think about the beauty of the world around me.

Think about the gorgeous ombre on a sunset on a random Tuesday.
Think about fields of colorful wildflowers dotting a landscape.
Think about the sweet smile on a newborn baby while they sleep.
Think about the constellations of stars that light up the sky every night.

There's beauty everywhere. And it doesn't always have a reason or a purpose or utility.

God has given us many creations that were made simply for the sake of beauty and enjoyment. Often, we can catch these glimpses as we experience nature. God takes time to beautify the world around us. Things that will not last forever, like flowers that are here today and gone tomorrow, are still intricately thought of and created (Luke 12:27–28).

Your creativity doesn't have to only be used in a way that is performative or useful—it can just be beautiful. Let go of your expectations about what will happen with what you make. Stop thinking about business, or if things are productive and marketable, or if they have a deep meaning.

Sometimes you have to just create to create.

Take inspiration from watching other creators. I've found many artists online who create fun hashtags to share creative projects just for the sake of adding beauty, fun, and whimsy into the world. One hashtag I love to follow is called #FaceTheFoliage. It's inspired by one of my favorite designers, Justina Blakeney (@justinablakeney). It began as her own personal challenge to make faces and images by solely using leaves, flowers, branches, and other natural elements found while foraging. Her creative project reminded me that I can use what's around me to create and inspire others. What started as a relaxing and therapeutic outlet has grown to include hundreds of entries from across the globe.

Another example is Vanessa Rivera (@the_life_of_aivax), a mother who uses her photography and design skills to re-create storybook art with her family. She crafts complete scenes and uses Adobe Photoshop to enhance the images to look like she is on these fun story adventures with her kids. Her images inspire me to think outside the box and create in new ways.

Or even how Morgan Harper Nichols (@morganharpernichols) began asking followers to send in requests, and she began to create custom poetry to help comfort and encourage others while practicing her gift of words. There are a number of ways that we can be inspired to create for creativity's sake.

Creating to create helps bring freedom. It helps me to use my gift without holding unrealistic expectations and opens my mind to create with childlike wonder. It keeps us connected to new ideas and out-of-the-box thinking. For me, I was having a hard time opening my hands when it came to trying new mediums in art. When I had first started creating again, I worked a lot by hand and with watercolor, but I had put that aside to focus on learning digital illustration. I found that I had built up so much confidence as a digital artist that it then felt hard to explore other artistic mediums.

I felt a gentle nudge that it was time to explore again. It was time to take out the paints, time to use my hands, get messy, and make art away from my screen again.

I cringed inside after looking at my early attempts.

Sometimes it's hard to be new at something again. To learn a new medium, to go a different way than you thought. It's hard to have that feeling of being out of control or unsure of where it might lead. But I knew God was asking me to trust Him in my creativity again. To try something new and to travel to a new place with Him in my gifts.

As I dusted off the old watercolor notebook and started to freely just play in the paint again, I felt a weight lift off me. It was messy. It was lively. It was fun. It was its own little journey on that page. It brought back a hope and excitement to make. I was filled with ideas again and it brought fuel to my creative fire.

So, friend, remember to stop and get out of your head with all the heavy questions and doubts. Allow yourself the freedom to create just to create. Don't worry about where it's taking you. Have fun and stay open. Find your joy, explore something new, or pick up something you once put down.

It doesn't have to be useful; it can just be beautiful.

Affirmation

I can trust God's pace
in my life and
be free in my creativity.

Playlist

"What a Friend" by Chandler Moore

"What I'm Waiting For" by DOE

"Higher" by Madison Ryann Ward

"Need" by Ryan Ellis

Creative Assignment

Take a moment to reflect on your creative journey by browsing what you've created. That can be photos on your phone of your artwork, blog entries, or something else you've designed. Remember the process of creating each piece. How have you grown? What things have you learned? Take a minute and write out a note of celebration of your journey.

_____

_____

_____

_____

_____

_____

_____

_____

_____

_____

Wonder and Reflect

Think of a time where you had to wait for something your heart truly desired. What helped you while you waited?

_____

_____

_____

What are some moments you can remember from your journey that show you how far you've come?

_____

_____

_____

Name any big or small victories you have experienced recently. How can you celebrate those wins?

_____

_____

_____

_____

_____

_____

_____

Prayer

Lord, I thank You for the gift of creativity. As I use my creativity, please help me to release my expectation and take pleasure in simply bringing beauty into the world. Help me to trust Your pace for growing my gifts and to enjoy celebrating each win. I know when I look back, I will see Your fingerprints all over my life. Amen.

Express Yourself Here

Finding What's True

Lies can come in many different forms. Clients will be dishonest, imposter voices will feed you lies, and sometimes when your projects are rejected, you can start to believe that there is something wrong with you. When these things happen, ask God to point you toward what's true.

Overcoming Lies with Truth

IN 2023, I was invited by W Hotel to speak on a panel called What She Said. The event is a global initiative to get changemaking women together for a night of community sharing stories and insights. Featured guests have included several bold and ambitious women from across the globe, all from various backgrounds—amazing women including director Ava Duvernay, fashion designer Diane von Furstenberg, and singer LeToya Luckett.

The panel I was on included all local Black women from various industries. Our panel comprised successful business owners and community builders, each doing major work in local entertainment, wellness, arts, and social initiatives. Each one had broken past barriers in their careers and had been lauded for courageously showing up to lead the way in their industries and communities.

I was incredibly honored to join in on the panel but couldn't help but feel a bit overwhelmed. Anytime I am invited to speak on a panel or share my story, it makes me a little nervous. Doubt tries to creep in and tell me that I am not really supposed to be there.

But when doubt started to creep in, I knew what I needed to do. I needed to get out of my head. As I sat with sweaty palms, I began to speak faith over my heart.

"You are exactly where you're supposed to be," I whispered to myself. "All you need to do is be yourself. Be real and God's gonna do the rest."

The night went smoothly as we each shared our stories, lessons learned, challenges and wins.

Closing out the night, the host asked for audience questions. A young woman, who looked to be in her twenties, was at the back of the room and raised her hand. I noticed that she was one of the women who had been taking professional photos throughout the night. As she made her way to the mic, she explained that she had recently started pursuing her photography business full-time, and it had been filled with so many ups and downs.

As she finished her story, she looked at each of us and asked, "When did each of you stop feeling imposter syndrome? When did you start feeling fully confident in yourself and what you create and do?" The other panelists and I looked at each other, grinning. It felt like we all wanted to tell her the same thing.

You don't.

Even when you have a track record of success, comparison can still creep in. Imposter syndrome had just reared its head earlier that night. Although I had a number of successes in my career and had achieved many things I never thought I would, I still had moments where I felt inadequate or that I didn't belong. Moments when I felt like I needed to accomplish more, or when I felt like what I did accomplish didn't measure up to others.

There might not be ways to avoid feeling like a fraud or like you don't deserve a seat at some tables or stages. But it's encouraging to know that even when these feelings creep in, you can confidently show up anyway.

I was able to speak truth over myself the day of that event because years earlier, I had started making a list based on Romans 10:17: "So then faith *comes* by hearing, and hearing by the word of God" (NKJV).

shine
bright.

One side of my list was labeled "truth" and the other was labeled "lie." I started with all the negative thoughts that were holding me back and added them to the "lie" column. Then I spent time adding to the truth side. I'd use scriptures, affirmations, quotes, or words I personally received from loved ones or from the Lord. For example, it might look like this:

Lie:

I am not creative.
I'm not good enough.

Truth:

I was made in the image of God (Genesis 1:27).
He has given me gifts to glorify Him (1 Peter 4:10–11).
I was made to do good works (Ephesians 2:10).
He is with me and will help and strengthen me (Isaiah 41:10).

When I finished, I'd read it aloud to myself so I could hear the truths and God's Word. This practice gave me peace and I added to it regularly.

I'd hang the list at my desk to look at as I worked. When I'd be drawing and have moments of doubt, I'd look up at the list and speak as many truths as I needed to hear to keep going.

Soon the truth side was filled with so much more to hold on to. The lies seemed big to me at first, but they never measured up to all the truths. This little tool helped me to unravel those lies I was believing. It helped me to break up with the lies, and I made it a habit to declare truth over my heart. I began to know the Word of God more deeply, and this practice totally transformed my faith and boosted my confidence.

As the truth of God's Word pierces through the lies and strengthens your heart, may you be encouraged in your creativity and trust in the gifts you hold. May you tap into your faith to believe, even in the darkest of moments, that He works all things together for good.

Do something today that builds your confidence in who God made you to be. You are enough. Overcome the lies of the imposter with truth.

You might start with making a list, like I did. Or you might reach out to a friend and ask for a word of encouragement. Or perhaps listen to encouraging words in a sermon or inspiring podcast to help push you toward confidence. Whatever encourages your faith, as you implement it, you can be sure of God's Word and the promises and plans He has for you.

The Sting of Rejection

ABOUT THREE YEARS into my business, my older sister started sharing some opportunities of other ways to finance and support my art career. She's always been a resourceful person and I'm sure that was part of the reason, but she also saw my struggle to grow a business with babies on the hip and the uphill climb that it was. She'd heard my complaints about finances, time, and the stress of starting a new career. One idea was to apply for grant funds through our state's artist community.

The idea of applying for a grant felt very out of reach. *No one is going to pick me*, I thought. I knew other people had received them, I'd even remembered kids getting grants for college, but I had never secured a grant for myself.

"Aren't those hard to get?" I asked her. I was already counting myself out. I had met the minimum qualifications, but still that didn't feel like enough.

Why would they choose me?

I was self-taught, a mother of two, and I didn't go to a professional school with renowned artists. I worked from my kitchen table in between naptimes. I did not think I was the type of candidate that the artist community supported.

Right then my sister reminded me, like she always did, "*Someone is* going to get it. And that *someone* could definitely be *you*."

I realized that I definitely couldn't win if I didn't at least put my name in the hat. Without an example to guide me, I blundered my way through the questions, feeling more unqualified the further along I went. But I hit Submit anyway.

Ok, I did it.

I also sealed it with a prayer asking God to grant me favor with the decision-makers.

Grants often take months to be reviewed and sometimes even a year before you get the funds, so I waited with so much anticipation, watching the board meeting schedule for their review dates and listening in on board meetings. Finally, the day came when an email arrived in my inbox from the grantor. I closed my eyes, took a deep breath, said "Please, God," and opened my email.

"We regret to inform you" was all I needed to see. I couldn't really process everything else the letter said. I didn't get it and I was defeated. Though I hadn't been confident I'd get the grant in the first place, I still wasn't prepared for the sting of rejection. To add insult to injury, the email came with a file of a short recording for me to listen in as the judging board reviewed my application. I didn't want to listen to the critiques of why I failed and so I didn't at first.

It would be weeks before I pressed Play. When I did listen to their ideas, I was frustrated because I felt misunderstood in my application. Right away all the discouraging voices I had heard over the years came bubbling back into my mind.

I remembered the anxiety of twelve-year-old me feeling insecure about my art and comparing myself to others. I thought of the doubt I heard in some friends' voices when I told them I was leaving my full-time job to take this leap. It all came back like a flood over my mind.

They hadn't picked me. It stung again.

I was mad that I had let down my guard and upset at myself for getting my hopes up. The rejection felt like a personal attack. A you-are-not-good-enough message in

"Don't you dare
give up."

my inbox. My eyes filled with tears and my heart filled with uncertainty. Was I really an artist? Did I really belong in the artist community?

Disappointment has a way of trying to take us off course from where we are headed. Rejection begins to feed us lies that we were never enough. It can touch a nerve in old wounds that we'd forgotten and thought were healed.

Whether it's being denied an artist grant, not landing the client we want, or seeing negative comments or critiques about our work posted online, we are going to face moments where it's hard to push forward. Anytime you put yourself out there, you are opening the door to the possibility to hear no or "we've decided to go with another candidate."

Have you ever felt discouraged because of a project? Maybe like me, you've felt like giving up? Throwing in the towel? Have you tried to perfect a recipe and just can't figure out what you're doing wrong? Or you've gotten feedback on your design project that you just don't agree with? Maybe you've wanted to walk away and set it down. It feels too hard to keep going.

I am here to encourage you to just keep going. Don't you dare give up.

I know these feelings of rejection are going to keep showing up in my art life. You and I will, no doubt, encounter moments where it feels easier to turn around and go back or we want to throw in the towel.

Through the years, there have been a few key ideas and mindset shifts that helped me to dig in and push forward. I hope they help you when you face rejection.

Realize that rejection and setbacks are part of the process of putting yourself out there and creating. Not everything you do and create is going to wow and amaze others. You will experience moments when you feel like you have failed or when you don't meet the mark, but rejection and noes do not define you. They are not a measure of your value or importance. See them as another part of the growth process. Reframe your thinking to accept obstacles as learning opportunities rather than failures.

After hearing criticism, take time to reflect on it objectively. Try not to take it personally and instead ask yourself, *What can I learn from this?* In your quiet, vulnerable moments with God, ask Him what He would like you to take away from this experience.

Lastly, getting up and trying again is going to benefit you in the long run. You are going to fall down more times than you can anticipate. And though I did eventually go on to receive that same grant after my rejected application (yay!), what helped me was listening to feedback objectively and trying again. Adapting to an attitude of perseverance will help you get out of your head and get back in the game.

So don't you dare give up.

Aligned

THESE NEXT FEW pages will focus a bit more on business, but even if you don't own a business, this is still for you! What I've learned on the business side has also helped on my personal life and art. Even with my business degree and corporate experience, running my own business felt brand-new. But what I didn't have in entrepreneurship experience, I had in passion and drive for creativity and art. I loved the making, painting, and creative time much more than the business side, but I knew that could get me only so far.

One thing I learned early on was the importance of communication and contracts. As an artist, it was important to explicitly set out the terms that would govern the job. The client needed to know up front the number of edits included, a clear description of how we will work together, a timeline for feedback, and what they could expect for the deliverable. They also needed to know what additional charges they would incur if they wanted to keep making changes.

But not every situation can be controlled with a contract. Sometimes you will just have difficult or unpleasant people to work with. Sometimes you won't see it coming. At times you will ignore all the bad-client red flags because you have bills to pay. No matter how careful you are, sooner or later you will run into an undesirable situation, and you'll count the days until the project is completed.

At times it may be hard to determine if the opportunities presented to you are in alignment with your personal values.

When I am first approached by a potential client, I take out my detective hat and research them online. I browse their social media accounts to determine if they are

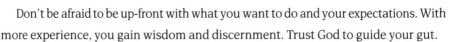

really who they say they are. I believe that if the organization is serious about representation in their advertising, then it's important that diversity is reflected among the decision-makers as well.

As a creative, I like to work with organizations that are innovative and fun. I try to imagine the synergy between us or how our two businesses could work together. What relationship could we build? I always ask clients, "What made you reach out to me? Give me some examples of what drew you to my work."

Don't be afraid to be up-front with what you want to do and your expectations. With more experience, you gain wisdom and discernment. Trust God to guide your gut.

Sometimes that involves saying no to clients that aren't the best fit.

I have had freelance jobs where there were red flags that I ignored and lived to regret it. They may be nice and well meaning, but maybe you get a weird feeling or just a gut response that something is off. Your body often tells you what your brain doesn't want to see. It might be uncomfortable to say no or turn down the offer, but you will know inside it's the right thing to do.

I was pleasantly surprised to get an email from a corporate client that wanted to hire me to create artwork centered on uplifting Black people and Black voices. It was a cool opportunity, and I'd get the chance to work with a large brand I hadn't worked with before. At first glance, the project aligned with the work I do and care about.

My first red flag was that the rates they were offering were much lower than what was standard in the industry. While I have had my fair share of conversations negotiating rates and know that it's part of the process of closing a deal, that was one area that just didn't feel right. I felt lowballed. What I was asking for was fair. Despite my better judgment, I decided to move forward with the contract because it still presented a great opportunity to get my foot in the door with this national brand.

Once the contract was signed, I noticed that the tone and friendliness with the account managers shifted. While the team said they supported me as a mother and artist, their actions said otherwise. Deadlines were contrary to industry norms, and they were clear that they expected immediate responses to emails, many which were

you made the stars
and know me by
name

sent during weekends, nights, and holidays—all things that encroached on my personal and work boundaries. The final red flag was they would fail to mention things that I needed to do in the initial scope and began adding additional work.

At first, I tried to be easy and generous and agreed to help with some of these pieces, but the more I said yes, the further away we got from what was in the scope of the contract. I had to put my foot down and began calling it out so that they would pay me for the additional work. I started having an uneasy feeling every time I would get an email from them. It often made me anxious. This was a sign. My body was telling me something was off about this business relationship.

In the end, sales exceeded their goals, and the client enthusiastically invited me back for another project. Knowing the terrible experience I'd had working with this client, I should have never considered the offer, at any price. My mental health and well-being were more important than going through this experience again. But in that moment, I thought, *If the pay is right, I'll consider it.* If I took the job, I planned to set my boundaries early on.

When I suggested a higher rate, the account manager's mood shifted.

"I'll check with my boss," she said coldly.

I knew then that I needed to listen to the signs. That was the final red flag. I knew that no matter what answer she came back with, my answer would be "Thanks but no thanks." I had to trust my gut and take a minute to think about why this experience had been so miserable. Beyond money and logistics, the experience showed that they didn't genuinely respect me as a professional or value my work.

It was clear to me that this company was not who I wanted to be aligned with. I wasn't sure if they cared about uplifting my voice, as they initially claimed. It felt like bait and switch. I felt like they used my Blackness and creativity to perform allyship for their own financial gain. It felt dishonest to be in collaboration with a client that did not practice what they preached. I didn't like how that felt. And I was glad for that clarity.

With confidence, days later, I declined their offer to continue working together.

As creatives, we are optimistic and hope for the best. Our life's passion is to bring beauty and light into the world, but sometimes things can get messy.

Even when you ask God for discernment, you won't always see the red flags clearly. Sometimes your judgment will be clouded by your need to pay the bills or your desire for greater opportunities. But even when you feel stuck in a bad situation, you can trust God to show you the way forward. It's never too late to stand up for yourself and live out your values.

You won't always know the end from the beginning with every important decision. But you don't have to. God knows. Believe that God's gentle hand will guide you through, even when you've made choices you regret. He's got this.

Affirmation

I can overcome lies with truth.

Playlist

"Unstoppable" by Koryn Hawthorne

"Jireh (My Provider)" by Limoblaze, Lecrae, and Happi

"Man of Your Word" by Maverick City Music

"And You Don't Stop" by The Walls Group

"Wake Up" by Terrian

"Stand Strong" by Sunday Service Choir

Creative Assignment

What lies from the imposter are you struggling with today? Take some time to creatively express the truths that combat those lies. Display your creation in a spot that will remind you of truth every day. I would love to see your creativity shine; post a picture on social media and tag @spoonfuloffaithstudio.

_____

_____

_____

_____

_____

_____

_____

_____

Wonder and Reflect

What questions should you ask a client to determine if your values are in alignment?

_____

_____

_____

As you use your creative gifts, how can your faith encourage you and give you confidence?

_____

_____

_____

What has helped you in the past when you've wanted to give up?

_____

_____

_____

Take a moment to think about a time when you felt stuck in a business relationship that turned sour. How did God help you get out of that situation? What did you learn?

_____

_____

_____

_____

Prayer

Lord, I thank You for all the people You have put in my path to help me learn and grow. Help me to silence the imposter's voice with truth from Your Word. Help me to "not allow ourselves to get fatigued doing good. At the right time we will harvest a good crop if we don't give up, or quit" (Galatians 6:9, MSG). Give me the clarity, focus, and strength to keep walking forward even as things feel difficult. Amen.

Express Yourself Here

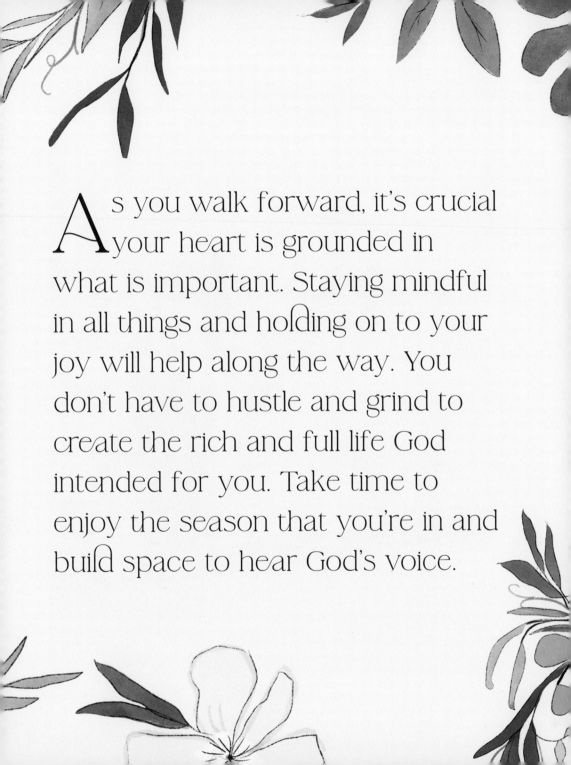

As you walk forward, it's crucial your heart is grounded in what is important. Staying mindful in all things and holding on to your joy will help along the way. You don't have to hustle and grind to create the rich and full life God intended for you. Take time to enjoy the season that you're in and build space to hear God's voice.

New
Perspective

AS AN ARTIST, I like to imagine and think of ways my art could live out in the world around me. I've always had a love and passion for beautiful products, but there was one canvas I hadn't tried after years of creating digital art: public art and, more specifically, a mural. It became a goal I felt ready to tackle. What would it look like to have one of my illustrations on a large scale? Up until then, I had mostly created on a small scale and never anything larger that 20x24 inches.

I decided to make my own creative challenge to inspire me and encourage my faith to believe that one day I could get a job for a mural. Looking around, I didn't have any spare walls to use, so I had to get creative. I started searching for blank walls around my home, local shops, and in community spaces. When I'd find a good one, I would snap a photo in front of it. I would use that photo as my canvas and dream up ideas for what a mural might look like in that actual space. I used my digital art tools on my iPad to create a mock-up mural idea on the photo.

In the process of creating a mock-up, I began to understand how tough this project would be. I would have to look at my art from a new perspective, literally. Painting a mural involves much more planning for intentional placing of the various elements. I had to look at my art in a completely different way. It was intimidating and, at the same time, invigorating to become a beginner again.

Would the mural include lettering? Where would I place them so that people could stand to take selfies or group photos and the words wouldn't be lost? I worried about getting proportions correct and choosing the right colors to create interest and dimension.

Once my mock-up looked how I wanted it, I shared it online with friends, family, and my Instagram community. I paired it with a caption sharing my desire to grow my gift of creativity in a new way and my hope to one day paint a mural. I signed it with the hashtag #JenaDoesMurals.

Next up was thinking about logistics.

How long would it take to complete and how much would I charge for something like this? What if the idea didn't look good in the space? How would I sketch it out to see the artwork to scale? Did I need an assistant to help me? I noticed very quickly that the planning portion was a lot of work. There was so much to think about when it came to not only the wall itself but even the environment around it. It felt very different than when it was just me, my paint, and my page.

And who was going to be the first to let this beginner paint on their wall?

While I didn't immediately book a job to do a mural, that simple act of starting to draw and believe for murals helped to pave the way for me. What I initially thought would happen "someday" came sooner than expected. People encouraged me through comments and messages. Within a few months, I heard from friends who wanted to help. They connected me with other muralists who shared their tips with me. About one year later, I landed a few mural jobs. Through this simple challenge I pushed myself to do, I was able to inspire, design, and paint multiple large-scale murals.

It's okay to be nervous or unsure about new things. The adrenaline reminds us of the beauty of being alive. Moments filled with energy and Holy Spirit wind are exactly what we need to keep living this adventurous life with God. When we remember what we've learned, remember Who we can lean on, and Who propels us forward, it gives us a new perspective.

" It's okay to be nervous or unsure about new things."

Have you ever felt stuck or nervous as you try new things in your creativity? Maybe you want to try out something new but the butterflies in your stomach are holding you back? Maybe your insecurities start to bubble up, telling you that you could never do it?

Every time I find myself in any of those places, I tell myself that it's an invitation to be brave. In that moment, I get to use what I've learned and to trust God in a new way. I also found that when I used my gift of creativity, I was able to document the uncomfortable process of trusting Him in the unknown in a unique way. I've documented these times through writing, my gratitude journal, my lies and truths lists, and creative challenges. Creative challenges, like #JenaDoesMurals, are one of my favorite ways to do this.

Take a moment to think about this creative adventure you're on. Your creativity can live in the world in a hundred different ways. Give yourself a few minutes to visualize how your work can expand and be used or show up differently than it has in the past.

How can you try something new to gain a new perspective on your creative work?

Document your process and have fun challenging yourself to try something new.

Making Space

GOD WANTS TO use every unique gift. Know that His plan won't deplete you or have you running on empty. You are not designed to run on empty.

I admit I love working and getting things done. But if I am not careful in setting healthy boundaries for myself, it quickly leads me to burnout. I'll become irritable, have less patience with everyone around me, and find myself feeling stuck in my ideas or not able to break through creative blocks. Then I get resentful because I'll feel like I'm doing so much work but barely making any progress.

I've had to be especially mindful about overworking because when I go too hard, my body retaliates. Lupus causes inflammatory flare-ups, and I can feel run down and exhausted in my joints and body. When I reach that stage, I *can't* work. And then I feel even further behind, do not give myself enough time to fully recover, and start the cycle of pushing too hard all over again. Maybe you've been there before, too?

It was in one of those burnout seasons that I received the invitation that my soul needed. A friend, Manda Carpenter, who I'd met through the good ol' internet, had just written a devotional called *Space*. She messaged me to let me know she'd be coming to town to host a workshop for her book and wanted to meet me.

Excited to finally connect in person, I messaged my sister-in-law and asked if she wanted to join me for a little girl time. I knew it would be a life-giving event for us to

do together. What I didn't realize was that making time to attend would stir something in my heart that I still hold on to today.

The workshop was specifically on creating space. It was geared toward women who were tired and busy and longing for healthier ways and rhythms to live their lives. *How did she know I needed this?* As the event began, Manda shared her story of living in a state of hustle and how God helped her to break free from it.

I felt so refreshed after the event. But there was still so much I needed to learn. As I got home and worked through the devotional, many things continued to shift in my mind. One major takeaway was that God desires our lives to have healthy rhythms to them. We were never created to be overrun and worn down. God wants us to live lives that reflect healthy habits.

I began to discover that creating a healthy flow in my life meant making sure I prioritized space and creating margin in my days. I had to do personal inventory. What was I really spending my time on? I had desired to be an entrepreneur for freedom to be with my family, but my calendar did not represent that at all. I wanted to be an ambitious creative, but rarely was I spending time to experience the world, gain inspiration, or explore. I started to make a conscious effort to ask myself questions about everything I'd added into my life.

Does this fit our family's rhythm?
Does it align with my vision?
Is it life-giving?
Will it take precious time away that I need elsewhere?
Is it draining us?

By removing things that did not align with my priorities, I found more freedom in my days.

The more space we make, the more we see God show up in the in-between. When we have the time, He presents more opportunities for us to participate in the good works around us.

For me that looked like Sunday brunch at the table with our family and praying together. Or a free afternoon that gave me time to give helpful advice when a friend called. It meant taking care of myself by tending to my body—stretching, meditating, and resting. When I made space, I finally had the ability to say yes to God for whatever the opportunity. I was available for the interruptions God wanted me to tend to. It allowed the Holy Spirit to do whatever He wanted to do with that space.

When there were things I couldn't remove, I tried to think more consciously as I scheduled for the future. I no longer took meetings or had deadlines on certain days of the week. I stopped responding to emails on the weekend or working after business

hours. While my days didn't grow extra hours, I found more intention with the hours I had. By giving myself permission to say no to things that didn't align with the rhythm I wanted, I also enjoyed more breathing room and a better pace for my days.

What else can happen to our creativity when we make space?

As I kept making space, I began to see its effects trickle into all areas of my life along with my creative work. Prioritizing space gave me time to sit, explore, experience the beauty of life, and gather inspiration that fed me creatively. As I used my gifts, inspiration came easier because I was creating from a healthy rhythm in my life. This caused deeper connection and confidence as I created.

With each minute gained, each morning slowed, I was getting my life back. I began to see everything shift a little each day. I had the ability to be present with God and with those in my life. My work felt more focused and in alignment with the life I desired. Making space and living from a healthier rhythm brought meaning back to every part of my life.

Don't get me wrong, life be lifing. You will inevitably encounter busy seasons. In the same month that you have major deadlines, a family member will have a medical emergency, you'll have car trouble, your kid's team will win a big game, and suddenly you'll have extra tournaments on the weekend. There's no way around it. You might have to come back to these reminders, again. But taking the time to be mindful about making space can help us get back on track even when life throws us off course.

How often have you felt run down by all the things you feel you have to do? Maybe you know that you need a healthier rhythm to your life but don't know where to start? Or maybe you struggle with having a healthy schedule and feel like you fail with every attempt? Sometimes just having simple steps forward is all we need to start implementing a more intentional rhythm.

- Take a moment to review what is holding you back or the obstacles you face. You will have a clearer vision of your starting point.
- Sit down and figure out if your schedule is aligning with your priorities and values. If creativity is important to you or there's a skill you'd like to practice, you'll need to make time for it.
- None of us has extra hours to add to the day, right? Start by reviewing things on your plate that you might remove to free up more time. You can use the questions I mentioned earlier or come up with questions of your own. For those items that no longer align, it may be time to make shifts in your life that will allow for better time spent on higher priorities.
- As you create space, show up to those moments open to what will come from it. It doesn't have to be a lot of time, but enter into it with the intention to use it well. Maybe there's been something you've wanted to explore and now's your moment. Or maybe you ask God to show you how to spend the time or you simply use it as a place to pause and be.

As you open yourself to making space and allowing God to fill it, He will show up in new, unexplainable ways. Let God fill you with confidence in trusting that when we trust Him with our time, He will guide and take care of us. As we make space, we get to experience more intention in everything we do, including our creativity. God will increase your capacity to love and serve others through the space made and help you to maintain a healthy rhythm of life.

Where
Your Feet
Are

BETWEEN OCTOBER AND December, during the height of sweater weather, boots, and pumpkin-flavored brews, every creative business owner or shop is fervently working on making all the gifts in time for the holidays. If you have a creative business, you're hopefully ahead of the game, but if you are like many of us (aka: me), you start to drown in the busiest season of the year.

For several early years of my business, I inevitably tried to get ahead of the holiday rush but failed. I wanted to spend time with my family but was stuck like glue to my office. I didn't want to miss out on the holiday break with my kids. But I knew the routine: My children would get a couple weeks off school, and I'd be overwhelmed because I didn't have the time or headspace to spend it with them. I'd feel guilty and try to cram in events and traditions, but my mind was never present and always somewhere else. Every spare moment would be filled with checking my emails, responding to customer requests in the corner of the room, and completely missing it all. Did we do all the traditions? Check. Did everyone have fun? Not really. Did we feel restful as we went about the season? Almost never. My people got the rest of me and not the best of what I could give.

The final straw was during our family vacation a few years ago in Florida for the holidays. I was stuck finishing up an art piece for a client on Christmas Eve. All of my immediate family—my siblings, their kids, and my parents—were there. My husband had the kids out back in the pool playing, and everyone was enjoying their time away. I had locked myself in the bedroom with my iPad so I could work through a few final orders. I kept trying to put it down, but I had to get it done. I'd be up most of the night finishing. My kids were growing up so quickly and I was missing moments with them. I knew in that moment something needed to change. I was missing planned family vacation memory moments. Ugh, not okay.

"The grass can grow and flowers can bloom right where you are."

For years, I had felt God's pulls and nudges leading me to rest more. So, the following December I decided to close my retail shop midmonth. Closing before the holidays felt not only countercultural but also counterproductive. Quarter four is where many businesses make their biggest profits. It's when customers are ready to buy without much prompting. I'll be honest, I stressed about how much money I would lose by shutting down during the busiest season all the way through the holidays.

But, as I closed my shop, I felt an immense burden began to lift. I knew my husband and I would make it work and that it was worth it for my mental health. It was a hard choice to make, but as I took it one step at a time, I knew this change was needed and in the long run would be a much better plan for our family, and I would never have a repeat of that prior Christmas.

Have you been in a place where you don't feel present? Sometimes it feels like the grass is greener on the other side, but the truth is the grass can grow and flowers can bloom right where you are. Don't get so carried away with creating that you miss the beauty of your present moments.

You can start by focusing on showing up right in your own home, relationships, and community. Day by day, I started practicing mindfulness in all I did. Whenever I would find myself rushed or worried, I would sit with both my feet on the ground and take three deep breaths until my mind was present with where I was physically. This helped me to recenter and reminded my heart to bring my full self to wherever I was. Take time to sit in the present, whether that's with family, friends, or alone. It also helped me to remember to trust the path that I knew God had set me on.

I began to focus on what I had been taking for granted: my relationships and support system. I worked on calling and checking in on friends and family more. I planned more intentional time with all my people. I scheduled date nights to get time away with my husband. I planned a coffee date and art exhibit visit with a friend. I connected with my kids and sat down with them more. I used my creative gifts to make crafts and love on them in ways they needed. Take a moment to think of some creative ways you can be more intentional with your relationships and support system. Try to get time scheduled in the next month.

Being mindful in your life can help you connect more with others, their needs, and how your light and gifts might be able to help serve or help those around you. As you connect deeper, your heart can be filled with more ideas and creative ways to show up authentically in your world.

God takes careful thought about each gift He's placed within us. We have the opportunity to steward our gifts well to create the life we want. These gifts aren't given to us to be a burden. Remember that when you Do It as Worship, you are trusting God with the outcome. You can be mindful and present. You don't have to hustle and miss out on the beauty around you.

Friend, wherever God has planted you—in your relationships, family, and community—is good ground and deserves your love, energy, and attention. Don't neglect the gardens you've been given. God has placed you strategically and has given your life purpose and promise where you stand. Tend to your garden well and stay focused on where your feet are.

When Artists Go to Work

I DIDN'T FEEL inspired. It was 2020, after all.

We were facing a global pandemic that was reporting thousands of deaths daily, the gravity of our country's social injustice toward Black people was inescapable, and our daily routines were dramatically changed forever with no end in sight. We were stuck. Stuck in our homes physically and forced to do life differently. Our family had been impacted deeply, losing people we knew and loved that year. This compacted my hopelessness. I'm sure you vividly remember that year as well.

Each day I would wake up early and have just about an hour to make my coffee and go to my home office to journal and get a list going for my day. I'd have to mentally prepare myself for the reality of being stuck at home and helping my six-year-old daughter with distance learning. My son, just in preschool, was my tagalong on most days, so I'd plan to do some learning activities with him throughout the day as well. The day was filled with stops and starts, as I was constantly moving from mom, to artist, to business owner, to teacher, and more.

My husband still went into work during this time, so as soon as he would come through the door, I'd pass the baton and try to will myself to get to the work I couldn't get to during the day. When I'd get this moment to create, nothing would come out. There'd be a war inside of me. *Why does any of this matter anyway?* The world felt on fire. We were stuck in the house, trying to stay safe and trying to carry on as usual. Everything had changed in my plans. I was angry and upset. Frustrated. Creativity didn't really feel like it mattered and even if it did, I couldn't access it.

During my quiet time, I connected with the Lord through praying and journaling, but even then, most of my prayers were groans. If they weren't groans, they were cries, yells, and screams at all of my frustrations.

Despite all of this, I created one of my favorite illustrations right in the middle of that year.

As I was trying to come up with ideas for a piece for a client, I felt inspired to create something that exuded joy. It was the opposite of the way I felt most days. I thought back to a conference I attended a year earlier, where I heard from author and poet Renée Watson. In her talk to writers, storytellers, and illustrators, she reminded us that no matter what we face, we must "remember joy and that it is a form of resistance" (SCBWI Conference, August 2019, Los Angeles, Invited Talk).

That stuck with me. During one of the most chaotic times in my life, my creating, my story, my art, my joy, and showing up in that was a form of resistance. It was not time to throw in the towel or to feel like my art was frivolous, but to channel those deep feelings to keep pushing forward and keep creating. It reminded me of the following powerful quote from Toni Morrison. These words she wrote back in 2015 still speak to the past, present, and future when facing despair:

Do not forget the importance of your joy.

This is precisely the time when artists go to work. There is no time for despair, no place for self-pity, no need for silence, no room for fear. We speak, we write, we do language. That is how civilizations heal. I know the world is bruised and bleeding, and though it is important not to ignore its pain, it is also critical to refuse to succumb to its malevolence. Like failure, chaos contains information that can lead to knowledge—even wisdom. Like art.

–Toni Morrison, "No Place for Self-Pity, No Room for Fear,"
The Nation (March 23, 2015)

Her words inspired me. As I sat and reflected, I thought of so many others before me who had to face times of chaos, uncertainty, and hopelessness. In that very moment in my office, I remembered I had access to deep joy. My joy was a form of resistance. It was a way to get back up. To hold on. It was something I found through my faith and that no one could ever take from my ancestors or from me. I knew I had work to do, to pull myself out of this place. And so, I decided to create a piece to remind me of joy.

I took out my tablet and began to draw. As I created, I thought about joy and hope, and I let my pencil flow where it needed to flow.

The painting itself shows the image of a face of a woman with closed eyes. Beneath and around her are flowers blooming and flowing onto the other side. The background behind her is painted in a light blue with words written in the sky: "Do not forget the importance of your joy."

Joy isn't dependent on only good things taking place. "Good" art has never only shown up in good times. When the world is bruised and bleeding, we cannot be overcome by it. This is the time we create to process, to heal, to persevere. As I created, I prayed all those who would come across my work would be inspired to find faith through it, and take it as permission to go and create, to process, and to heal in their own way.

You have creative permission to connect with hope in your own unique way as you walk through difficult seasons. In your creativity, reach for joy. In your worship, reach for compassion. Create and make from the sincere gratitude of all God has brought you through.

Do not allow your trials to turn off the deep-rooted well of strength inside of you. Dig deeper and remember your resistance. Remember, creating in times of difficulty is precisely the work God's given you to do.

"You have creative permission to connect with hope."

Affirmation

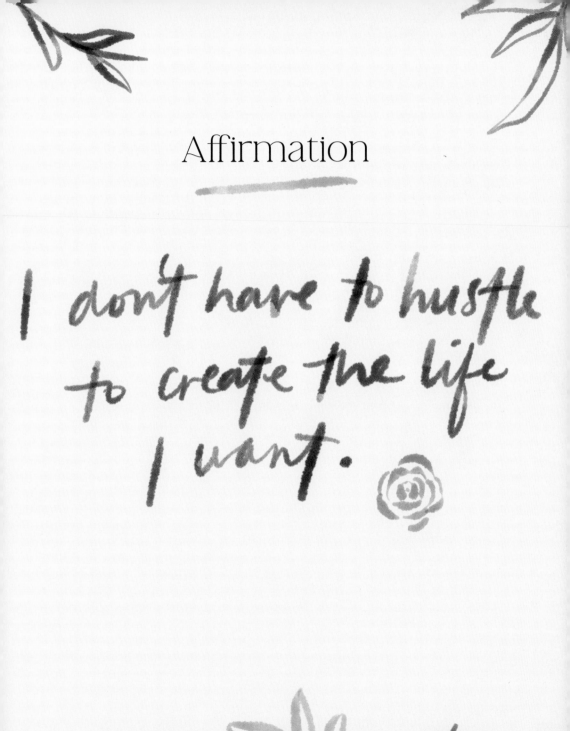

I don't have to hustle to create the life I want.

Playlist

"Mighty You Are" by The Walls Group

"More Than Anything" by Sunday Service Choir

"Love & Adoration" by Madison Ryann Ward

"Beautiful" by Hulvey

Creative Assignment

Over the next week, focus on being mindful throughout your day. As you go about your routine, stop and write down what inspires you in your notebook or phone. Take a moment to reflect at the end of the week. What days felt hard to feel inspired? Why? What moments were especially inspiring? Are there any themes arising in where you find inspiration? Use your findings to help prompt your next creative session.

_____

_____

_____

_____

_____

_____

_____

_____

_____

_____

Wonder and Reflect

Take a moment to take inventory of your life. Are you burning out? Are you enjoying your creative work? Are God's gifts feeling like a burden? Ask God to help you be mindful about the life you're creating and the margins you can create.

_____

_____

_____

_____

What specific ways can you encourage yourself as you step out into new places?

_____

_____

_____

_____

_____

Take a moment to think about a time when you felt stuck in a business relationship that turned sour. How did God help you get out of that situation? What did you learn?

_____

_____

_____

_____

_____

Prayer

Dear Lord, give me eyes to interpret the season I am in and wisdom to be present with where I am. You have placed us in our relationships, families, communities, and in this time in history. You know what we face daily and You have given us these creative gifts to bring beauty, hope, and joy in chaotic times. Anchor us in Your love and purpose for our lives. Help us to remember that Your gifts are not a burden, and we can find unique ways to build margin and space in our lives.

Express Yourself Here

God Is Faithful

I SAT ON the black stool and began to spin around. As I twirled, I saw a blur of colors from all of the artwork hanging from the walls and craft supplies in various bins around me. When I stopped, I sat in awe. It was mine; this little studio space I was twirling around in was something I could call my own. It was a small space nestled in the middle of a larger shared studio, with a few other artists. My space was right next to a great window with incredible light. I had been there about a year, but every time I came there, I thought of God's faithfulness to me.

There have been all types of small memories, art pieces, mementos, and more that I have held on to over the years because they marked how God had been faithful. This dedicated studio meant so much more than a space for me to work in. It was a constant reminder of all that I had walked through to get to this place, all God had brought me through and showed me along the way, how His faithfulness had turned many of my little dreams to reality.

I remember when I had first begun using my creative gifts and practicing illustration, I mentioned the nudge to create to a good friend, Tawni, who is also an artist. She immediately encouraged me in my faith and told me to go for it. A week later, I came home to a package at my doorstep. When I opened it, inside was a Wacom tablet, a gift from her. I had been eyeing this illustration tool for months. With tears in my eyes, I called her to express my gratitude. She told me that God had put it on her heart

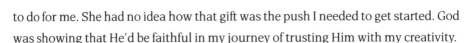

to do for me. She had no idea how that gift was the push I needed to get started. God was showing that He'd be faithful in my journey of trusting Him with my creativity.

I spent several years working from the kitchen table, the office I had created in my bedroom closet, or anywhere I could find myself enough space to make. Twirling in my chair in that studio was monumental to me. What may seem small to some—one-fifth of a shared space on the third floor of the building—was huge to me. It mattered. It mattered because the journey to get there mattered. It was a gift to me from God.

This shared space also meant so much because of how I had struggled with connecting with the local arts community. I didn't know if I would belong. I had my own insecurities of fitting in to a community that felt tight-knit. I felt like an outsider because I came from the world of motherhood and marketing and was self-taught.

While it was awesome growing from a small Etsy shop to major brand partnerships with retailers like Target, Michael's, JOANN, and Aerie, and to press features in *Essence*, Buzzfeed, Huffington Post, *People Magazine*, and *Good Morning America*, my art didn't have the same connection locally.

It felt easier to stay in my little bubble and create in my own little corner of the world. It was working for me! But I got out of my shell to connect with others. I was introduced to communities of small-business owners, creatives, artist directories. I found business associations like Women's Venture and industry groups like SCBWI, Highlights Foundation, and local artist collectives in Minneapolis, such as NEMAA.

As I look to the future, I am excited to see where my creativity will grow. I have big ideas, such as building a community center for arts. It feels like a huge mountain to climb, but I never want to stop dreaming with God. I never want to lose the wonder of creating, inventing, and innovating together. The joy that I have found in walking hand in hand with God as I use my creativity, has truly changed my life. Whether it be through a whisper from God, a closed door, something I listen to, or a loved one's words or actions, I'm determined to follow the big and small ways that He'll lead me. I'm trusting that whatever adventure lies ahead, it will be more fulfilling than I can expect.

"Remember His faithfulness, trust His resume, and look toward your future with hope."

Take a moment to look back over your life, not at your shortcomings, but at where you saw God show up. What have you walked through to get here? What ways have you seen opportunities or connections come through to show you that God has taken thought for you?

Now take a moment to look toward the future. What new ideas are brewing within your heart? What freedoms do you feel in your creativity? What lessons learned are helping to propel you forward?

Your gifts of creativity may not seem like much in your hands, but with God's plan they can bring healing, hope, and love to others. Stay willing and open to the journey. Trace His hand within each step and watch as what He's placed within you gets developed and shows up in extraordinary ways. Remember His faithfulness, trust His resume, and look toward your future with hope.

As you create by faith—picking up your brushes, your pens, your hands—you'll discover that God wants to teach, love, and transform you and the lives around you. It may feel like the messy middle, but He's not finished with any of us yet. Keep dreaming and putting passion into all you pursue. Walk confidently with the evidence of His resume and create from a place of joyful worship, knowing that if you just show up as your unique self, with all He's given you, it can be used for His glory.

PRAYER:

Lord, help me to look back from where I've come and see Your hand of faithfulness. Illuminate the ways in which You have been ever present. As I continue to walk forward in faith, help me to stay confident in Your resume. Amen.

Acknowledgments

This book has been in my heart for many years. I doubted if I could actually see it to the end. I would be lost without the help of all of those in my corner, my village, holding my hands up when I felt I couldn't. In big ways and small, your support has been what has made this dream a reality.

To my husband, Adrian, who has kept me grounded but also stood with me through the roller coaster of it all, helping to hold down the fort and reminding me of the importance of us doing it all as a team. To Layla and A. J., who in more ways than they will ever know are the constant motivation to everything I get the opportunity to create. Thank you for your patience when I work and your kindness when I just need a hug.

To my mom and dad, whose words and wisdom have held me together—teaching me through faith and affirmation that I am exactly who God created me to be. Mom, your words of affirmations often carried me through this book-writing process. Thank you both for all you've imparted in my life and for gifting me Truth.

To my brothers and my sisters—Nisha, Naya, Nanca, Wade, Jerry, and Loryn— thank you for always being there. And for not being afraid to use your gifts in your own unique ways. Your creativity has stretched mine to believe in six times more possibility in the world around me. Thank you for encouraging creativity in your children as well. To my nieces and nephews, you each inspire me by how you live out your potential and walk forward boldly as the next generation.

To Ashley and Tawni, friends who spoke life to my ideas from the very start, nine years ago. Aisha, thank you for the coffee chats, three-hour phone calls, and constant support that I always feel from our time spent together near or far. JAMM, who helped encourage me to keep going every time I wanted to give up at the end and being the first to remind me to celebrate the victory of finishing. To the twenty women who trusted me to lead a group on creativity amid my doubts. To all the children at Woodland Elementary who told me they wanted me to make more books, your seeds of encouragement truly mean so much to me.

To Jenni Burke, my incredible agent, who saw the story in me and helped me to believe it was worth sharing. To the incredible team at WaterBrook Multnomah—Jamie and Kim and the countless hours you helped to tweak and make this come to life. Thank you for believing in my story. To the design team for championing my vision and trusting in my ideas. Delina, for your coaching and reminders of the power of my authentic voice and letting it appear on these pages.

To all my friends, family, and supporters who've cheered me on, purchased my work, championed my voice, and shared my art or hung it on the walls of your home, I couldn't have done it without your faith in me. And to Sarah, Melarie, Luana, Dara, you all personally have made a special impact on my journey.

Dear Lord, I am continually in awe of the ways You create new beginnings within my life. I am eternally grateful and ready for whatever You are up to creating next. Here's to the next adventure!

Jena Holliday is a full-time artist, writer, entrepreneur, and storyteller from Minnesota. She is the creator and owner of Spoonful of Faith illustration and design studio, as well as the author and illustrator of the children's book *A Spoonful of Faith*.

With just a bit of faith, she walked away from her mainstream marketing job to embrace her passion for art. What started as a hobby eventually evolved into a full-time commitment of spreading kindness and hope through her artwork and words. That commitment blossomed into a blog and shop, aptly named Spoonful of Faith, and has become not only a successful business but also a cultural beacon.

Holliday wants her journey and her illustrations to motivate others, especially women, to face fear, find their voice, and use it to walk boldly in all God has for them.

spoonfuloffaith.com
Instagram: @aspoonfuloffaith / @spoonfuloffaithstudio